SELECTED OTHER BOOKS BY THICH NHAT HANH

No Death, No Fear

Living Buddha, Living Christ

Peace Is Every Step

The Blooming of the Lotus

Being Peace

Breathe! You Are Alive

The Heart of Understanding

Interbeing

The Miracle of Mindfulness

Old Path, White Clouds

Present Moment Wonderful Moment

Zen Poems

CREATING TRUE PEACE

Ending Violence in Yourself, Your Family, Your Community, and the World

THICH NHAT HANH

FREE PRESS
New York · London · Toronto · Sydney · Singapore

*f*P

FREE PRESS
A Division of Simon & Schuster, Inc.
1230 Avenue of the Americas
New York, NY 10020

FREE PRESS and colophon are trademarks
of Simon & Schuster, Inc.

For information regarding special discounts for bulk purchases,
please contact Simon & Schuster Special Sales:
1-800-456-6798 or business@simonandschuster.com

"Recommendation" from *Being Peace* by Thich Nhat Hanh.
Copyright 1987, 1996, by the Unified Buddhist Church, Inc.

Designed by Dana Sloan

Manufactured in the United States of America

1   3   5   7   9   10   8   6   4   2

Library of Congress Cataloging-in-Publication Data

Nhât Hanh, Thích
Creating true peace : ending violence in yourself, your family,
your community, and the world / Thich Nhat Hanh.
p.   cm.
1. Peace—Religious aspects—Buddhism.
2. Buddhism—Social aspects.   I. Title.
BQ4570.P4.N45   2003
294.3'37873—dc21   2003049162

ISBN 0-7432-4519-9

CONTENTS

Chapter One: WHAT IS TRUE PEACE?   I

Chapter Two: TURNING ARROWS INTO FLOWERS:
Practicing Inner Transformation   11

Chapter Three: PEACE BEGINS WITH US:
Taking Your Practice into the World   54

Chapter Four: RIGHT ACTION COMES FROM RIGHT
UNDERSTANDING   85

Chapter Five: RECONCILIATION:
Peace Practices for Individuals and Partners   110

Chapter Six: TO LOVE MEANS TO BE TRULY PRESENT:
Practicing Peace with Your Child   141

Chapter Seven: PROTECTING PEACE:
Community and Sangha Practices   168

Chapter Eight: A CALL FOR GREAT COMPASSION   182

EPILOGUE:
*A New Global Ethic: Manifesto for a
Culture of Peace and Nonviolence*   207

CREATING TRUE PEACE

CHAPTER ONE

WHAT IS TRUE PEACE?

True peace is always possible. Yet it requires strength and practice, particularly in times of great difficulty. To some, peace and nonviolence are synonymous with passivity and weakness. In truth, practicing peace and nonviolence is far from passive. To practice peace, to make peace alive in us, is to actively cultivate understanding, love, and compassion, even in the face of misperception and conflict. Practicing peace, especially in times of war, requires courage.

All of us can practice nonviolence. We begin by recognizing that, in the depths of our consciousness, we have both the seeds of compassion and the seeds of violence. We become aware that our mind is like a garden that contains all kinds of seeds: seeds of understanding, seeds of forgiveness, seeds of mindfulness, and also seeds of ignorance, fear, and hatred. We realize that, at any given moment, we can behave with either violence or compassion, depending on the strength of these seeds within us.

When the seeds of anger, violence, and fear are watered in us several times a day, they will grow stronger. Then we are unable to be happy, unable to accept ourselves; we suffer and we make those around us suffer. Yet when we know how to cultivate the seeds of love, compassion, and understanding in us every day, those seeds will become stronger, and the seeds of violence and hatred will become weaker and weaker. We know that if we water the seeds of anger, violence, and fear in us, we will lose our peace and our stability. We will suffer and we will make those around us suffer. But if we cultivate the seeds of compassion, we nourish peace within us and around us. With this understanding, we are already on the path of creating peace.

The teachings of this book are offered to help anyone who aspires to lead a life of nonviolence. These practices are the living legacy of the Buddha and of my ancestral teachers. They are as powerful today as they were at the time of the Buddha's awakening, 2,600 years ago. Together, they form a practical manual of peace—for you, your family, your community, and the world. At this time, with so much conflict in the world, I am offering this book to help us realize that violence is not inevitable. Peace is there for us in every moment. It is our choice.

The Nature of War

In 1946, during the French-Indochina War, I was a novice monk at the Tu Hieu Temple in Hue, central Vietnam. At that time, the city of Hue was occupied by the French army. One day, two French soldiers arrived at our temple. While one stayed in the jeep outside the temple gate, the other came in, carrying a gun, and demanded all of our rice. We had only one sack of rice for all the monks and he wanted to take it away. The soldier was young, about twenty, and hungry. He looked thin and pale, as if he had malaria, which I also had at that time. I had to obey his order to carry our heavy bag of rice to the jeep. It was a long distance, and as I staggered under the bag's precious weight, anger and unhappiness rose up in me. They were taking the little rice we had, leaving our community without any food. Later, to my relief, I learned that one of the older monks had buried a large container of rice on the temple grounds, deep in the earth.

Many times over the years I have meditated on this French soldier. I have seen that, in his teens, he had to leave his parents, brothers, sisters, and friends to travel across the world to Vietnam, where he faced the horrors of killing my countrymen or being killed. I have often wondered whether the soldier survived and was able to return home to his parents. It is very likely that he did not survive. The French-Indochina War lasted many years, ending only with the French defeat at Dien Bien Phu and the Geneva Accord in 1954. After looking deeply, I came to realize that the Vietnamese were not the only victims of the war; the French soldiers were victims as well. With this insight, I no longer had any anger toward the young soldier. Compassion for him was born in me, and I only wished him well.

I did not know the French soldier's name and he did not know mine, but when we met we were already enemies. He came and was prepared to kill me for our food, and I had to comply with his order to protect myself and my fellow monks. The two of us were not, by nature, enemies. Under different circumstances, we could have become close friends, even loving each other as brothers. It was only the war that separated us and brought violence between us.

This is the nature of war: it turns us into enemies. People who have never met kill each other out of fear. War creates so much suffering—children become orphans, entire cities and villages are destroyed. All who suffer through these conflicts are victims. Coming from a background of such devastation and suffering, having experienced the French-Indochina War and the Vietnam War, I have the deep aspiration to prevent war from ever happening again.

It is my prayer that nations will no longer send their young people to fight each other, not even in the name of peace. I do not accept the concept of a war for peace, a "just war," as I also cannot accept the concept of "just slavery," "just hatred," or "just racism." During the wars in Vietnam, my friends and I declared ourselves neutral; we took no sides and we had no enemies, North or South, French, American, or Vietnamese. We saw that the first victim of war is the person who perpetrates it. As Mahatma Gandhi said, "An eye for an eye only makes the whole world blind."

The Nature of Peace

During the war in Vietnam, those of us who practiced nonviolence learned that it is truly possible to live happily and free from hatred, even among people who hate us. But to do so, we need to be calm, to see clearly what the real situation is and what it is not, and then to wake up and act with courage. Peace is not simply the absence of violence; it is the cultivation of understanding, insight, and compassion, combined with action. Peace is the practice of mindfulness, the practice of being aware of our thoughts, our actions, and the consequences of our actions. Mindfulness is at once simple and profound. When we are mindful and cultivate compassion in our daily lives, we diminish violence each day. We have a positive effect on our family, friends, and society.

Some people think there is a difference between mindfulness and meditation, but this is not correct. The practice of mindfulness is simply to bring awareness into each moment of our lives. Mindful living is an art. You do not have to be a monk or live in a monastery to practice mindfulness. You can practice it anytime, while driving your car or doing housework. Driving in mindfulness will make the time in your car joyful, and it will also help you avoid accidents. You can use the red traffic light as a signal of mindfulness, reminding you to stop and enjoy your breathing. Similarly, when you do the dishes after dinner, you can practice mindful breathing so the time of dish washing is pleasant and meaningful. Do not feel you have to rush. If you hurry, you waste the time of dish washing. The time you spend washing dishes and doing all your other everyday tasks is precious. It is a time for being alive. When you practice mindful living, peace will bloom during your daily activities.

Please use the guided meditations in this book to help you practice mindfulness and nonviolence. You can use these practices individually, and you and your family can enjoy them together. These step-by-step meditations help us to calm our emotions and to see our "interbeing"—to see that there is no separation between you and me, between you and any other person, to see that we all "inter-are." As my friend Martin Luther King Jr. wrote, "All life is interrelated. We are all caught in an inescapable network of mutuality, tied into a single garment of destiny."

The spiritual teachings of all traditions help us cultivate the seeds of compassion, nonviolence, inclusiveness, and reconciliation. They show us the way out of fear and conflict: Hatred cannot be stopped by hatred. Violence should not be responded to with violence. The only way out of violence and conflict is for us to embrace the practice of peace, to think and act with compassion, love, and understanding. Yet many of us have lost faith in these teachings and think that they are unrealistic and outdated. Instead, we invest ourselves in the pursuit of fame and wealth, thinking that these will make us happy. When we are honest with ourselves and look deeply into our hearts, however, we will see that even if we had unlimited wealth and power, we could still live in fear. The only way out of violence and conflict is for us to embrace the practice of peace, to think and act with compassion, love, and understanding.

A Personal Peace Treaty

Included in these pages are examples of agreements that you can make with yourself, your partner, and your family. These treaties commit us to practice reconciliation and communication with loved ones, friends, colleagues, and other people with whom we live and work. They are concrete commitments to transform our lives.

To make a personal peace treaty we can write: "Dear Self, I promise to practice and live my daily life in a way that will not touch or water the seed of violence within me." We are determined in every moment to protect ourselves from negative thinking and to nourish loving-kindness within us. We can also share this commitment with our beloved ones. We can go to our partner, our son or daughter, and say, "My dear, my beloved one, if you really love me, please do not water the seed of violence in me. Please water the seed of compassion in me. I promise to do the same for you."

You can honor this commitment in many ways. You can avoid situations that make you angry or create conflict with others. For instance, when you read a magazine you may encounter ideas and images that water the seeds of hatred and fear in you. Or while you are conversing with someone, the discussion may make you upset and you may feel anger rise up in you. During these moments, your practice is to become aware that the inner seeds of anger, fear, and hatred are being watered and that these emotions can lead to violence in your thinking, in your speech, and in your actions. Please put away any reading material that does not nurture love and understanding. Please avoid taking part in conversations that water negative seeds in you. Let your beloved ones know how they can support you in preventing irritation and anger from growing in you.

In a similar way, you can support your beloved ones in the practice of peace. When they share with you what makes them sad, angry, or depressed, take note, and with kindness act in their best interests. Try to avoid doing or saying things that you know will water the seeds of conflict within them. This is a concrete, intelligent way to practice peace.

Many young people alive today have not endured the great pain of war. They do not remember the horrors brought about by mass violence. We must help our children awaken to the fact that they have within themselves the capacity for violence and war as well as the capacity for caring and loving-kindness. With mindfulness, we must also teach our children concrete practices that nourish the positive seeds within them and avoid strengthening the negative seeds of anger, craving, and fear. We should begin this learning process when our children are young so that as they grow they have the strength and skill to be calm and to act nonviolently and insightfully.

Before he died, the Buddha instructed his disciples, "Be a lamp unto yourself." In this way, he urges each of us to light the lamp of mindfulness in our own hearts. My dear friends, let us practice energetically so that we may light the way of peace for our beloved ones, for our society, and for future generations.

From Commitment to Action

As a young monk at the Buddhist Institute in Vietnam in the 1940s, I had a deep aspiration to put into action the beautiful teachings of the Buddha that I had received. I had become a monk because of my ideals of service and compassion, but I was deeply disappointed that I had not found the opportunity to express those ideals in the monastic life as we lived it then.

At that time, our country was under foreign rule. We lived in the midst of war and oppression. Yet the teachings and practice offered to us at the Buddhist Institute did not seem to correspond to the reality of our situation. Many of us young people wanted to help others and to respond to the injustice in our society. Many were attracted by Communism because it seemed that the Communist Party offered a real chance to serve our people. So many young people joined the Communists with this sincere aspiration and a beautiful desire to help only to find themselves fighting and killing their own brothers and sisters.

Fortunately, at that time I was in touch with the writings and teachings of some senior Buddhist monks who showed me the path of peace and nonviolence in the Buddhist tradition. I left the Buddhist Institute because I did not find an appropriate teaching and practice there for responding to the reality of life in Vietnam, but I did not leave monastic life. I stayed a monk and over time, together with like-minded friends, created a small community that combined the practice of mindfulness and dwelling peacefully in the moment with social work. In this way, we helped to initiate the movement of Engaged Buddhism, and our community offered support to the people and villages suffering from the war and political oppression.

Words and thoughts concerning compassionate action that are not put into practice are like beautiful flowers that are colorful but have no fragrance. The practice of mindfulness is already the action of peace. The practice of mindfulness has the power to transform us and to affect the whole world. We have to practice the cultivation of peace individually and in our relationships. We need to practice peace with our partner, children, friends, neighbors, and society. Only this kind of practice will allow the flower of peace to take root in our families, in our communities, and in the world. Each one of us can draw from the wisdom of his or her own spiritual tradition—whether it is Judaism, Islam, Christianity, Buddhism, or any other.

We must examine the way we consume, the way we work, the way we treat people in order to see whether our daily life expresses the spirit of peace and reconciliation, or whether we are doing the opposite. This is the practice of deep looking that will make peace possible in our daily life. There is hope for future generations only if we can put into practice our deep aspiration for a culture of peace and nonviolence. If we cannot take practical measures to bring about a global ethic of nonviolence, we will not have enough strength to face and deal with the difficulties we will encounter in this new century. We can do this. True peace is possible.

Dear Reader, as you read this book, please do so with the understanding that peace is already here and now. It is already a part of you. Please read these pages slowly and calmly, so that the very act of reading is peace. Remember, the practice of peace always begins right here, right now.

CHAPTER TWO

TURNING ARROWS INTO FLOWERS

PRACTICING INNER TRANSFORMATION

Violence is never far. It is possible to identify the seeds of violence in our everyday thoughts, speech, and actions. We can find these seeds in our own minds, in our attitudes, and in our fears and anxieties about ourselves and others. Thinking itself can be violent, and violent thoughts can lead us to speak and act violently. In this way, the violence in our minds manifests in the world.

The daily wars that occur within our thoughts and within our families have everything to do with the wars fought between peoples and nations throughout the world. The conviction that we know the truth and that those who do not share our beliefs are wrong has caused a lot of harm. When we believe something to be the absolute truth, we have become caught in our own views. If we believe, for instance, that Buddhism is the only way to happiness, we may be practicing a kind of violence by discriminating against and excluding those who follow other spiritual paths. When we are caught in our views, we are not seeing and understanding in accord with reality. Being caught in our views can be very dangerous and block the opportunity for us to gain a deeper wisdom.

We usually think of violence and war as an act or event with a definite beginning and a definite end. But when we look into the true nature of war, we see that, whether war breaks out or not, the seeds of war are already here. We do not have to wait until war is officially declared to recognize its presence. When the opposing armies have left the battlefield and gone home, it seems that war no longer exists, but that may not really be true. The war may still be there. Although the fighting has ended, hatred and fear are still there in the hearts and minds of the soldiers and the soldiers' fellow citizens. The war is there, yes, and if we look around we will recognize its many faces: religious intolerance, ethnic hatred, child neglect, racial discrimination, and exploitation of the world's resources. But we also know that the seeds of peace, understanding, and love are there and that they will grow if we cultivate them.

When we recognize the violence that has taken root within us, in the everyday way we think, speak, and act, we can wake up and live in a new way. We can make a strong determination to live mindfully, to live in peace. Shining the light of awareness on the roots of violence within our own hearts and thoughts, we can stop the war where it begins, in our minds. Stopping the war in our minds and in our hearts, we will surely know how to stop the war outside.

Turning Arrows into Flowers

The night before his enlightenment, the Buddha was attacked by Mara, the Tempter, the Evil One. Mara and his army of demons shot thousands of arrows at the Buddha, but as the arrows neared him, they turned into flowers and fell harmlessly at his feet.

This is a powerful image. We can all practice so that we can receive the violent words and actions aimed at us and, like the Buddha, transform them into flowers. The power of understanding and compassion gives us the ability to do this. We can all make flowers out of arrows.

During the war in Vietnam, one of my closest students, Sister Chan Khong, who was also a professor at a university in Saigon, wrote a petition for peace. She persuaded seventy of her fellow teachers to sign it. Shortly afterward, there were widespread attacks on South Vietnam by troops from the North, and the atmosphere became very tense. As a result, the local authorities made a public broadcast calling all the professors who had signed the petition to come to the Ministry of Education to sign a statement recanting their support for the peace petition. All of the professors except Sister Chan Khong complied.

The Sister was called in to speak with the minister himself, who said that if she did not withdraw her statement for peace, she would lose her position at the university and possibly be put in jail. Using her mindfulness training, Sister Chan Khong calmed her emotions and declared that she was determined to bear all responsibility for her act of initiating the petition. Then, she said, "Mr. Minister, as a teacher I believe the most important thing we can do during this time of killing and confusion is to speak out with courage, understanding, and love. That is a precious gift that we can give to our students. That is what I did. You, the Minister of Education, were a teacher, too, before having a high position in the government. You are like a big brother to us younger teachers."

When he heard this, the minister's heart softened. He understood and apologized and did not take any more action against Sister Chan Khong.

It is possible to water the seed of compassion even in such a situation of adversity. When we see clearly with the eyes and heart of understanding and compassion, we no longer feel that we are the victims of the other's violence. We can even open the heart of the person we feel is trying to hurt us. We can turn our enemies into friends.

As you begin your practice of nonviolence, this may seem very difficult to do. You become aware that violence is all around you. You become aware of the seeds of anger, fear, and hatred in your own consciousness. You may feel a huge block of suffering inside you and feel that you are unable to transform the anger and fear within you and the violence that is directed at you. For many of us this is the situation. We have allowed violence to accumulate in us for too long because we have had no strategy to deal with it. When we cannot handle our suffering, we spew forth our frustration and pain onto those around us. We are victims of our own suffering, but because we do not know how to handle it, we hurt others while we are in pain. We—each of us—must become responsible for our own pain and work to transform it in order to save ourselves and those we love.

As you begin to transform your own inner pain, you also transform other people's anger and hatred into flowers. You soon see that arrows shot at you come out of other people's pain. You do not feel injured by their arrows or actions; instead, you have only compassion. Your compassion transforms the speech and actions of the other person. Together these practices provide real self-protection, which is necessary before we can protect others.

Every time you smile away your irritation and anger, you achieve a victory for yourself and for humanity. Your smile is like the smile of the Buddha when he defeated Mara. Mara is within us in the form of suspicion, jealousy, and misperception, but with a good understanding of yourself and others, you will avoid getting caught by Mara and making mistakes. Instead of watering the seeds of violence, you will cultivate the seeds of compassion and bring relief to yourself and others.

Recognizing Everyday Violence, Acknowledging Our Suffering

An attitude of openness, the willingness to recognize and accept the diversity of human experience and the spiritual values of other traditions and cultures, is essential in the practice of nonviolence. We create true peace when we are inclusive of others. Yet inclusion and nonattachment to our opinions are sometimes difficult to practice. Exclusion, getting caught by our views, is a deep-seated habit that arises from fear and misunderstanding of others. To transform our habit of excluding others, we must practice and develop understanding and compassion in all parts of our life.

In some countries people are educated with force or violently indoctrinated against their wills. Many political regimes forbid their citizens to say or think anything other than official government propaganda. In these societies, there is no freedom of thought, expression, or action. This suppression is a kind of psychological violence. Many hundreds of millions of people in the world live in environments like this.

Unfortunately, many families operate in a similar way. For instance, in some cultures, boys are told by their fathers and society, "Men do not cry." They are taught to suppress their feelings, which is another subtle form of violence. As human beings, we suffer, and we should be allowed to acknowledge our feelings and, when we need to, say that we are hurting. We should allow ourselves to cry. Otherwise, we may become sick from suppressing our feelings.

When we hold back our feelings and ignore our pain, we are committing violence against ourselves. The practice of nonviolence is to be here, to be present, and to recognize our own pain or despair. We do not make war on our feelings or reject them, but just recognize, embrace, and transform them. When anger or fear is present in us, we bring awareness to it. We smile to it and call it by its true name. Hello, my fear, I know you are there. We can follow our mindful breathing to help calm our feeling. Breathing in, I am aware fear is present in me. Breathing out, I calm my feeling of fear.

When we don't acknowledge our feelings, the violence we do

to ourselves builds up within us. It can push us to lash out in anger, say destructive things, and hurt those around us, especially those who cannot defend themselves, our children. As parents and members of a community, we have to learn how to handle our anger without venting frustration on our children. Many families have been broken by violent speech, which has arisen out of the accumulation of violence inherited from parents, friends, and society.

Children accumulate emotional violence in both their bodies and their minds. If they do not know how to transform it, they may express it harmfully and lash out at others. Or, if they do not recognize it, they may repress it, creating a bomb, within themselves. Eventually, they direct the violence they feel at themselves in self-destructive ways. Many children feel they have no way to escape their pain, so they take drugs, abandon school, engage in reckless sex, or even commit suicide. Or they inflict suffering on themselves to punish those they believe have made them suffer. It is important to recognize our children's suffering and to act with compassion in order to help them recognize their feelings of anger, isolation, and fear. We can help them learn to be mindful. The energy of mindfulness is like a balm that can soothe and heal the wounds of hatred and suffering.

We are the continuation of our ancestors. We contain all the beautiful qualities and actions of our ancestors and also all their painful qualities. Knowing this, we can try our best to continue what is good and beautiful in our ancestors, and we will practice to transform the violence and pain passed down to us from so many generations. We know that we practice peace not only for ourselves but for the benefit of all our ancestors and all our descendants.

Key Mindfulness Practices That Cultivate Peace

Mindfulness is the foundation of happiness. A person who is unhappy cannot make peace. Individual happiness is the foundation for creating peace in the world. To bring about peace, our hearts must be peace.

Mindfulness is the practice of stopping and becoming aware of what we are thinking and doing. The more we are mindful of our thoughts, speech, and actions, the more concentration we develop. With concentration, insight into the nature of our own suffering and the suffering of others arises. We then know what to do and what not to do in order to live joyfully and in peace with our surroundings.

Two important practices that help us cultivate the energy of mindfulness are mindful breathing and mindful walking. Our breath and our steps are always with us, and we can use these simple everyday acts to calm our emotions and nourish our joy.

Mindful Breathing

To breathe in mindfully is to be aware that air is entering our body, and to breathe out mindfully is to know that air is leaving our body. The moment our mind is attentive to the contact between our body and the air, we are also in contact with our mind, just as it is. It takes only one conscious breath to be in touch with ourselves and the world around us. Then, with each mindful breath, ease is restored to our body and mind.

EXERCISE FOR MINDFUL BREATHING

To practice mindful breathing, just observe the natural rhythm of your breath. Please do so without forcing it to be longer, deeper, or slower. With attention and a little time, your breath will deepen naturally on its own. Occasionally, your mind will wander off. Our practice is simply to take note of this distraction and to bring our attention gently back to our breath. If you like, you may use the sentences listed here to help you in focusing your attention. During the duration of several in and out breaths, follow your breath from beginning to end. Use the keywords at the end of each pair of sentences to help you maintain your awareness:

1. Breathing in, I am aware only of my in breath. Breathing out, I am aware only of my out breath . . . In, Out
2. Breathing in, I am aware that my in breath grows deep. Breathing out, I am aware that my out breath grows deep . . . Deep, Deep
3. Breathing in, I am aware that my in breath goes slowly. Breathing out, I am aware that my out breath goes slowly . . . Slow, Slow

You can practice mindful breathing in any situation: while sitting, lying down, standing, driving, or working. Breathing consciously will bring more awareness and concentration to whatever you are doing.

Mindful Walking

Mindful walking is the simple act of being aware that you are walking. Instead of being carried away by your thinking, worries, or anxieties about the future or regrets about the past, dwell fully in the present moment, fully aware of each step you make. With each step, arrive in the present moment. You have already truly arrived, why are you still running? Whether you are walking down a street, into a building, or just from one side of a room to the other, be aware of the contact between your feet and the ground. Notice how many steps you make comfortably during an in breath and during an out breath. As you breathe in, say to yourself, "In," with each step you take. As you breathe out, say to yourself, "Out," with each step you take. You can practice walking meditation anytime during the day.

Mindful breathing and mindful walking are concrete ways to bring the practice of peace into your life. Using them helps you to defuse harmful emotions, calm and concentrate your mind, and bring yourself back to the present moment, where life is truly available.

By practicing mindful breathing and walking, we lay the foundation for mindful communication.

Speaking and Listening with Compassion

Today, communication between individuals, families, and nations has become very difficult. However, there are concrete ways to train ourselves to communicate nonviolently so that compassion for one another is awakened and mutual understanding becomes possible again.

Speaking and listening with compassion are the essential practices of nonviolent communication. Mindful communication means to be aware of what we are saying and to use conscious, loving speech. It also means listening deeply to the other person to hear what is being said and what is not being said. We can use these methods in any situation, at any time, wherever we are.

For our body to be healthy, our heart must pump a constant flow of blood. For our relationships to be healthy, we need a constant flow of mindful communication. Yet many people find it difficult to communicate effectively because they have so much frustration and anger built up inside. Even when we come to another person with sincere goodwill and the intention to listen, if we are unable to use calm, loving speech, there is no hope that the other person will hear us and understand what we are trying to say. We may intend to use calm and loving speech, but often as we start speaking, our pain, despair, and fear emerge. In spite of our best intentions, we start to blame, complain, and judge harshly. Our speech begins to reverberate with the kind of energy that turns people against us because they cannot bear to hear what we are saying. Communication breaks down. When this happens, we need to learn, or to relearn, how to communicate.

How then do we reach the point where we are able to listen deeply to one another and to use loving speech? To do this, we first have to practice taking care of our own pain and anger. By practicing mindful breathing and mindful walking, we strengthen the energy of mindfulness within us. We may need to practice and train ourselves for several weeks, or even several months, before we can overcome our pain and use loving speech.

When our mindfulness is strong, it is much easier to look deeply into a situation and to give rise to understanding and compassion. With the energy of mindfulness, we can overcome our pain and use loving speech.

The same is true about our ability to listen deeply. If we have not been able to embrace and transform our own hurt and anger, it will be difficult to listen to another person's suffering, especially if the other person's speech is full of negative judgments, misperceptions, and blaming. In our heart, we know that listening is what we should do, and no doubt we have often tried our best. Yet frequently, after a few minutes, we no longer can bear to listen to even one more word. We feel overwhelmed. Even though we have vowed that, regardless of the provocations or unjust assertions, we would stay and listen with compassion, we just cannot do it. Our good intentions evaporate because we are unable to handle the pain welling up within ourselves.

Yet if we can prevail and listen for only one hour, the other person will obtain a great deal of relief. Listening with an open heart, we are able to keep compassion alive. Then we give the other person a real chance to express his or her feelings.

Such listening requires training and practice. Along with the practices of mindful breathing and mindful walking, the following meditation can help transform the seeds of anger and irritation in us and allow us to open our hearts to listen with love and compassion to the other person.

MEDITATION FOR COMPASSIONATE LISTENING

1. Breathing in, I know that I am breathing in. Breathing out, I know that I am breathing out . . . In, Out

2. Breathing in, I calm my body. Breathing out, I smile . . . Calm, Smile

3. Breathing in, I know I have suffered. Breathing out, I smile with compassion . . . My suffering, Compassionate smile

4. Breathing in, I know you have suffered. Breathing out, I smile with compassion . . . Your suffering, Compassionate smile

5. Breathing in, I know we both suffer. Breathing out, I want us both to have a new chance . . . Our suffering, A new chance

6. Breathing in, I listen. Breathing out, I hear . . . Listening, Hearing

7. Breathing in, I hear your bitterness. Breathing out, I embrace you in my heart . . . Bitterness, Embrace you

8. Breathing in, I hear your wrong perception. Breathing out, I do not burn with anger . . . Wrong perception, Not burning

9. Breathing in, I know I have made you suffer. Breathing out, I am sorry . . . You suffered, I am sorry

10. Breathing in, I open my heart. Breathing out, in my heart there is room for you . . . Opening my heart, Room for you

11. Breathing in, I want to be happy. Breathing out, I want you to be happy . . . My happiness, Your happiness

12. Breathing in, I see us happy. Breathing out, that is all I want . . . Our happiness, Is all I want

At least one person in every family should be capable of loving communication. It can be a brother, sister, father, or mother. Is there someone in your family who can embody this kind of practice, someone who can help other family members practice deep listening and loving speech? Can you be this person? Can you be this person with your friends, in your church, synagogue, sangha, or community, or where you work? Perhaps there is a teacher in your child's school who listens with compassion and speaks without anger or judgment. The person who practices loving speech and deep listening is practicing peace. He or she opens the door for understanding, peace, and reconciliation to enter our hearts, our families, and our society.

In schools, in Congress, in city halls, in statehouses, we need people capable of practicing deep listening and loving speech. Unfortunately many of us have lost this capacity. To have peace, we must first have understanding, and understanding is not possible without gentle, loving communication. Therefore, restoring communication is an essential practice for peace. Communication is the foundation, the flowering of our practice of nonviolence.

The practice of mindful communication can also help us teach our children how to protect themselves and at the same time show them our faith in them. We can say, "My child, you will suffer if you speak in this way, and that is why you should be careful." Our children will understand. Trust in your children's wisdom and set a good example. If we as parents listen and speak mindfully, our children will learn to do the same. If we smoke, our children will smoke; if we drink alcohol, our children will also. If we talk and act violently, our children will, likewise, learn to be violent. We each have the responsibility to show the way of nonviolence, the way of compassion. We have to teach others by our way of living, not just by our words. If you do not know how to handle the anger and violence in yourself, it is impossible to help someone else, even your own child. Nonviolent action can be born only from nonviolent living.

When we see someone, especially a child, say or do something that is not to our liking, we easily become irritated. If our understanding and compassion are not strong enough to protect us, we will allow that person's behavior to provoke the seed of irritation within us. Consequently, what we say or do may be violent physically or emotionally. When you are irritated with someone else or with your child, you are not in a position to help or to teach him. At such a time, you have to refrain from saying or doing anything. Instead, please practice mindful walking, smiling, and mindful breathing and your peace and calm will be restored. When your calm has been restored, you will find the best way to approach the other person or your child and help her avoid doing or saying harmful things in the future. When you are lucid enough, you will not blame or punish but will handle the situation with understanding and love. This is taking good care of the seeds of anger and violence within you.

We all have the right to suffer, but none of us has the right not to practice. Our responsibility as humans is to transform our suffering in order to transform the suffering of those around us.

Transforming Your Suffering

To help befriend and embrace painful emotions, you may like to try the following meditations.

SMILING MEDITATION FOR EMBRACING AND
TRANSFORMING NEGATIVE EMOTIONS

1. Breathing in, I am aware of my body. Breathing out, I smile to my body.

2. Breathing in, I am aware of pain in my body. Breathing out, I smile to the pain in my body.

3. Breathing in, I am aware of pain in my mind. Breathing out, I smile to the pain in my mind.

4. Breathing in, I am aware of the feeling of fear in me. Breathing out, I smile to the feeling of fear in me.

5. Breathing in, I am aware of the feeling of insecurity in me. Breathing out, I smile to the feeling of insecurity in me.

6. Breathing in, I am aware of the feeling of sadness in me. Breathing out, I smile to the feeling of sadness in me.

7. Breathing in, I am aware of the feeling of anger in me. Breathing out, I smile to the feeling of anger in me.

8. Breathing in, I am aware of the feeling of jealousy in me. Breathing out, I smile to the feeling of jealousy in me.

When we have a positive feeling, we would like to keep that feeling as long as possible. The following meditation helps us to recognize and nourish the positive seeds within us:

MEDITATION FOR EMBRACING AND
NOURISHING POSITIVE EMOTIONS

1. Breathing in, I experience calm in me. Breathing out, I smile to the calm in me.

2. Breathing in, I experience joy in me. Breathing out, I smile to the joy in me.

3. Breathing in, I experience equanimity in me. Breathing out, I smile to the equanimity in me.

4. Breathing in, I experience openness in me. Breathing out, I smile to the openness in me.

5. Breathing in, I experience happiness in me. Breathing out, I smile to the happiness in me.

Practices to Protect Ourselves with Mindfulness

The practices in this chapter help to transform the seeds of violence within us and enable us to handle the violence directed at us. They help us to learn the art of protecting ourselves with mindfulness, which is the basis for being able to help others protect themselves. With these practices, your inner seed of violence stops growing, your seeds of compassion, equanimity, and loving-kindness increase. These are concrete practices you can use daily, throughout your life.

Learning the Earth's Practice of Equanimity

The Buddha taught Rahula, his own young son who became a monk, that the Earth could receive and transform anything that is poured on it. If you put garbage or waste on the Earth, she will receive it without being offended or repulsed. If we pour perfume, milk, or fragrant water onto the Earth, she does not become proud or arrogant. The Earth can turn what appears to be the most repulsive substance into beautiful flowers or delicious vegetables in just a few weeks. It is the virtue of the Earth to receive everything—ugly or beautiful—with equanimity. We should practice like the Earth.

Sometimes, even those people to whom we are closest pour anger, hatred, and misperceptions on us. Maybe you cannot yet receive and transform the hatred, anger, and misperceptions that others pour on you and you fight back. But if you remember that you are a son or daughter of the Earth, you can learn to be as she is—strong, constant, steady.

Please go back to Mother Earth and learn her way of receiving and transforming everything with equanimity. Each time you suffer, touch the Earth in your mind and say, "Earth, I suffer so much; please help me to receive this." You are not separate from her; you are the Earth herself. When you practice like this, you suffer less. When we learn the practice of equanimity from our mother Earth, we learn to accept all things. We do not suffer; we transform our pain, and on our face we have a loving smile for the person who has harmed us.

Recognizing Your Own Goodness: Your Buddha Nature

Sometimes a negative emotion arises in you and takes over. Something upsetting occupies your mind and you cannot let it go. Your feelings are like television channels; if you do not like the channel that is on, you can switch to another one. The Buddha called this the practice of "changing pegs," replacing a negative emotion with a positive one. A peg is a big wooden nail that is used to fasten two pieces of wood together. If the old peg is rotten, you drive it out by hammering in a new one.

Sometimes, however, when you try to replace a strong negative emotion with more positive thoughts or feelings, the first emotion keeps coming back. This can cause a struggle inside you. In such a situation, another way of dealing with your suffering is to recognize your capacity for being calm, for having understanding, compassion, and peace. This is your true nature, your Buddha nature, the awakened nature in you. When you bring to mind these qualities of great compassion and understanding, you acknowledge their presence within you and you will immediately suffer less.

Buddha nature is not an abstract notion. It is a reality you can touch and experience. Buddha nature exists in every cell of our body. The cells of our body are not made up of only physical matter. Our body is matter and it is also a manifestation of consciousness. The one contains the all, and each cell contains everything else. The infinitely small contains the infinitely large. Every cell of our body contains all the talent, wisdom, goodness, and happiness of the Buddha, and also of all our spiritual and blood ancestors.

Of course, every cell also contains within it the seeds of hell, of violence: jealousy, anger, and other negative emotions. But we can practice so that hell does not overpower the energies of mindfulness, understanding, and loving-kindness in us. When you are suffering, you forget your Buddha nature, your goodness, and believe that within you is only suffering, only fear, turmoil, and hatred. Please, remember to trust in your Buddha nature.

The Buddha had to face his own fear as he traveled the path of awakening. After the Buddha had turned away the arrows of Mara and his army of demons and transformed them into flowers, Mara appeared two more times. Having failed to sow doubt and fear in the Buddha's mind, Mara appeared to him in the form of the most beautiful of women, tempting him with desire in order to distract him from his purpose. The Buddha held up his hand and said, "You are just a distraction. You are not true." With that, the woman disappeared. Having failed to fill the Buddha with doubts and fear or desire, Mara then offered him unlimited earthly power and wealth. Again, the Buddha raised his hand and dismissed Mara and his offers as illusion. Each time Mara tried to tempt him, the Buddha brought his awareness back to his own goodness, named it, and by looking deeply and recognizing the illusions for what they were, overcame them.

WHEN YOU ARE in pain, remember to bring your mind back to your Buddha nature, your goodness and capacity for mindfulness, calm, and seeing deeply into the situation. If you allow yourself to be dominated by negative emotions, you will react in ways that will cause more suffering. You will want to punish the other person and say unkind things. We have all done this many, many times. To break out of this habit of suffering, this trap, we have to remember to practice mindfulness, to touch our Buddha nature.

Protecting our senses is a concrete way to nourish our Buddha nature. The Buddha taught that our six senses—eyes, ears, nose, tongue, body, and mind—are each like a deep ocean, filled with waves, monsters, and many hidden dangers waiting to overwhelm us. When we see an image, when we hear a sound, when we taste something, we can be carried away by our forgetfulness, our fear, and our craving. We lose our peace; we lose our capacity to understand and love. Unless we continually practice the cultivation of mindfulness, the light that guides our way, each sense, full of hidden dangers, can emerge and overwhelm us.

We all have negative emotions and we also all have Buddha nature within us, and it is possible for them to coexist in peace. The practice is to recognize our Buddha nature without running after it, and to recognize our negative emotions without running away from them. With mindfulness we can maintain our peace, our stability, and our compassion in every moment and in every circumstance.

MEDITATION FOR REMEMBERING YOUR GOODNESS AND BUDDHA NATURE

Even in the midst of suffering, it is possible to bring your awareness to the good qualities within yourself and allow them to manifest in your consciousness. Practice mindful breathing to remind yourself of your Buddha nature, of the great compassion and understanding in you.

- Breathing in, I am aware that I am breathing in. Breathing out, I am aware that I am breathing out.
- Breathing in, I am in touch with the energy of mindfulness in every cell of my body. Breathing out, I feel nourished by the energy of mindfulness in me.
- Breathing in, I am in touch with the energy of solidity in

every cell of my body. Breathing out, I feel nourished by the energy of solidity in me.

- Breathing in, I am in touch with the energy of wisdom in every cell of my body. Breathing out, I feel nourished by the energy of wisdom in me.

- Breathing in, I am in touch with the energy of compassion in every cell of my body. Breathing out, I feel nourished by the energy of compassion in me.

- Breathing in, I am in touch with the energy of peace in every cell of my body. Breathing out, I feel nourished by the energy of peace in me.

- Breathing in, I am in touch with the energy of freedom in every cell of my body. Breathing out, I feel nourished by the energy of freedom in me.

- Breathing in, I am in touch with the energy of awakening in every cell of my body. Breathing out, I feel nourished by the energy of awakening in me.

Continue to breathe like this for two or three minutes. Soon you will feel much better. You do not need to look more deeply than this. Simply trust in your own goodness, this is enough. Without struggling, allow your goodness to come back to you.

This practice is based not on notions or ideas but on the reality of your experience. In the past, we have all touched our own Buddha nature, our capacity for understanding and compassion, our ability to be calm, to look deeply, and we can rely on it in the present. Please do not work too hard at this or analyze it intellectually. Just place your trust in the goodness within yourself. Simply call on your Buddha nature for help.

Both our body and our consciousness have the wonderful ability to heal themselves. When you cut your finger and are in pain, you innately have confidence in your body's capacity to mend the cut. You do not have to do much: simply clean the cut and allow your body to do its work. The cut will heal on its own. The same thing is true with your consciousness, which has the capacity to heal, forgive, and generate goodness. You should recognize this capacity and affirm its presence in your body and consciousness. Develop faith in your own goodness, your own Buddha nature.

Sometimes when you are suffering, you think that living is impossible and you can't go on. When we lose a person who is very dear to us, we may think that we cannot survive. We feel we will die because we have lost our loved one. In time, however, we realize that we can go on living. Practicing mindfulness of our body and feelings, we feel better. The force of healing is always at work in us, and we must trust it. Our goodness, our ability to persevere, our capacity to let go and transcend will help us through.

The first property we purchased at Plum Village, our retreat center in rural France, was an old farm, which had on it about fifty-two acres of cultivated land and forty-eight acres of forest as well as many stone warehouses. We decided to plant 1,250 plum trees, the money for which was donated by the children who came to practice at our center. We planned to dry the plums to make prunes and also to make plum jams—all of which we would sell so that we could send the proceeds to hungry children around the world. That is the reason we named our center Plum Village. There were only few of us monastics there at that time, and we had to care for a number of Vietnamese refugees who were quite weak from their ordeals in the war and their travel to France. It was a lot of work to renovate this abandoned property and make it livable. An enormous amount of physical labor was required, and we also had to learn how to farm in a climate different from that of our native land.

We were blessed in having a neighbor who was a true angel, a bodhisattva, Mr. Mounet. The house he lived in was the original main house of the farmstead and was situated very close to us. He helped us a tremendous amount, lending us his tools, showing us what to plant and when, and he was always cheerful no matter what happened. Mr. Mounet was a big man and very strong. We depended on him, and we loved him very much.

One day I was shocked to hear that he had died of a heart attack, with no warning. We took a lot of care to prepare his funeral and to send our spiritual support and energy to him. One night I felt so pained by the loss of our friend that I could not sleep. As I was doing walking meditation to ease the sadness I felt at his death, the image of Mr. Mounet came into my mind. It was Mr. Mounet certainly, but not Mr. Mounet as I had known him. It was Mr. Mounet as a child, smiling the smile of the Buddha, happy and calm. It was Mr. Mounet's goodness smiling at me, still alive.

Please, do not think that because you are suffering you can speak harshly, retaliate, or punish others. You can still help others as you embrace the suffering inside you. Remember in those moments the Meditation for Remembering Your Buddha Nature. Breathe in and confirm your trust in your awakened nature, your capacity for calm and compassion.

Some people call this Buddha nature and capacity for compassion God. God may be a notion for some, but God as the energy of mindfulness, concentration, and compassion is not a notion. For me the energies of peace, wisdom, and stability are the energies of God, of the Holy Spirit. When we generate peace, loving-kindness, and understanding in ourselves, we are generating the energy of God within us. The next time you are troubled and upset and think you cannot survive, please use this simple breathing exercise to get back in touch with your own true nature, the nature of awakening and compassion. Please, do not give up. Mindfulness in action enables you to overcome all dangers.

The Lotus Can Grow Only from the Mud: Acceptance Practice

Being aware of our jealousy, judgments, and fear is already a positive step toward acceptance. When we accept ourselves as we are, we do not any longer need to fight to change ourselves. The moment we become aware that we are being too critical of ourselves and we accept our negative seeds, we are already making progress. People who are unaware of their negative energies will have difficulty making progress.

Even so, striving to increase our compassion does not mean that instantly there are only positive elements in us. If this were the case, there would be no need to practice. It is exactly because we have the seeds of negative energies in us that we continue to practice. The practice is easy: just become aware of our negative energies, and in just cultivating this awareness, we will make steady steps on the path. Conflict is not necessary.

We practice like the lotus flower and the mud. The lotus flower does not think, "I do not want the mud." The lotus knows that it can bloom beautifully only because of the mud. For us, the same is true. We have negative seeds within us, the element of mud; if we know how to accept this, we accept ourselves. The lotus flower does not need to get rid of the mud. Without mud, it will die.

Unless we have garbage, we cannot have flowers. We should not judge ourselves or others. We only need to practice acceptance and there will be progress without struggle. The process of transformation and healing requires ongoing practice. We produce garbage every day, so we need to practice continuously to take care of our garbage in order to make it into flowers.

There may be friends around us who seem to practice better than we do, but it is important to accept who we are and not reject ourselves or our efforts. If we have within us only 10 percent flowers and 90 percent garbage, we may wish we had 90 percent flowers and only 10 percent garbage, but this kind of thinking does not help. We have to accept the 90 percent garbage in us in order to be able to increase the 10 percent flowers to 12 percent, then 14 percent, and then 20 percent. This acceptance will bring us peace, and then we will not be caught in an inner struggle. Even those who produce many flowers daily have garbage and must practice continuously. It is okay for us to have the mud of suffering if we know how to practice. The Buddha said, "You cannot grow lotus on marble. You have to grow it in mud."

Even an enlightened person has to practice like this. You might wonder why a person who has accomplished so much still needs to practice. She does it in order to continue transforming the garbage. You might imagine an enlightened person is someone who does not need to practice anymore, but this is not true. She needs to practice to continue being happy, just as you and I do. She never stops practicing mindful breathing, smiling, and walking. This way she continues to generate within herself the flowers of joy.

SEVERAL YEARS AGO, while I was visiting Taiwan, I was walking down a dirt road with some friends. A mother and her young son were walking toward us on the opposite side of the road, holding hands. Our eyes met and I greeted him, placing my palms together, making a lotus bud with my hands in front of my heart in the traditional greeting, acknowledging the Buddha in him. With his mother still holding on to his hand, the boy smiled at me and, holding up his other hand in front of his chest, bowed and acknowledged the Buddha in me. Just after they passed, the little boy turned and looked back at us. His eyes widened, and it seemed to all of us as if he recognized me, and I felt we had met before. My friends and I stood watching as they walked away, out of sight.

I have on occasion thought of this sweet encounter as a lovely illustration of how we can all recognize the goodness and peace in each other. We are not strangers to each other. We are united by our Buddha nature.

The Mind of Love

Sometimes you encounter people who are so pure, beautiful, and content, they give you the impression that they are divine, that they actually are saints or holy beings. What you perceive in them is their awakened self, their Buddha nature, and what they reflect back to you is your own capacity of being awake.

There are genuine ways we can manifest our own Buddha nature. By touching our capacity for mindfulness through our thinking, words, and actions, we can increase peace and joy for ourselves and for others. By doing so, we nourish and protect the awakened nature of those around us.

However, you can also do the opposite. You can think, speak, and act in a way that touches your animal nature and awakens in others their animal nature. You may do this because you want to indulge your animal nature with them. Perhaps you want to make money with them in a not altogether ethical way, or you want to overeat or drink too much with them, or you want to have an illicit sexual relationship. You know it is wrong, but you do it anyway, causing suffering to yourself and those around you. Afterward, you wonder why you acted in this way, and promise not to do it again. But when the next time comes, you repeat the mistake, creating another circle of suffering. This cycle can become endless. You open the door of hell for yourself and others.

This is the condition for too many of us. For example, we may be tempted to eat a certain kind of food. We know that if we eat it, our body and mind will have a difficult time, but we indulge ourselves anyway. After we have suffered from indigestion, a hangover, or a heart attack, we promise that we will not do it again. Yet when the next opportunity arises, we repeat the same mistake. Some of us go to church or a temple to confess our wrongdoings and weaknesses, promise to do better, but commit the same kinds of mistakes and wrongdoings again and again. We are caught in a vicious circle.

The way to transcend this circle and avoid sinking in the ocean of our senses is to touch our Buddha nature and give rise to the Mind of Love, the mind of enlightenment, called Bodhicitta (pronounced: bo dee CHIT a). The great vow of the Buddha, Bodhicitta, is "With loving-kindness, I will help all beings to suffer less."

Bodhicitta is our great aspiration to wake up, to transform our suffering into compassion and serve all beings as a bodhisattva—a person of great compassion. You can make this great vow every day and give rise to the Mind of Love within yourself. You are motivated now by a deep desire to help all living beings transform their suffering and to bring them relief and happiness. Remember your Mind of Love whenever the desire arises in you to indulge in your animal nature. It may be the only thing that can rescue you. With it, you escape the vicious circle in which you have been caught all your life, and you now work to manifest Buddha nature, the awakened mind, in yourself and others.

Please, make this vow for yourself.

If we make a sincere effort to practice alleviating our inner suffering and the suffering of others, we too become bodhisattvas, awakened beings. We support our family, friends, and co-workers, and help them to manifest as bodhisattvas; we do this for the entire world and for the happiness of all beings. If through your practice you become a bodhisattva, those around you will see that beauty, genuine spirituality, and true love are possible. Living like this, you are happy, and will become an inspiration for others.

Allowing Buddha Nature to Embrace Animal Nature

Even when you have made your own vow to act from the Mind of Love, and sometimes you are successful in manifesting as a bodhisattva, other times your animal nature may take over. Nonetheless, you do not have to fight or kill the animal nature in you for your awakened or Buddha nature to reappear. Just smile to the animal nature in you and remember that compassion is always in you. Your Buddha nature will then embrace the animal nature inside with tenderness and mindfulness. This is a miracle—it allows your animal and Buddha natures to coexist in peace and harmony.

Remember, even the Buddha had animal nature in him. The only difference is that he knew perfectly well how to take care of it. All of us can learn to do the same. We cannot and should not try to kill the animal in us. We recognize our animal nature and vow to transform it; and we recognize our Buddha nature and vow to nourish it. We need only allow the Buddha nature in us to manifest and it will eclipse our animal nature. The desire to become an awakened person is strong in all of us. If we allow it to manifest, it will bring us—and many others—great happiness.

According to Buddhist teachings, there are ten realms of being or consciousness within us. When one realm manifests, the other nine are hidden. Among these ten are the hell and the animal realms, but there are also the Buddha, the bodhisattva, and the human realms. Think of your consciousness as a radio: there are many stations, but when one station is on, all the others disappear. You have the choice—you can choose a wholesome station or a toxic station. If you know the proper way to handle your body and mind, you can be your best for the sake of yourself and others. As you practice, you can stay more and more attuned to the Buddha and bodhisattva realms of consciousness.

Reconnecting with Ourselves: *Protecting Mind and Body*

By making the time to practice for yourself, you are not wasting your efforts; on the contrary, you are using your time wisely. The Buddha taught us not to neglect ourselves but to take care of ourselves. He encouraged us to practice intelligently, to look deeply into our suffering, and to take effective actions to transform it. To be helpful to others, you have to give yourself permission to practice for yourself; you cannot neglect yourself. No one is more worthy of your kindness and compassion than you are.

All the exercises in this chapter—breathing, smiling, deep relaxation, and the others—help you reconnect to yourself and to practice peace. As you do them, listen to your body and listen to your consciousness. When we reconnect with ourselves, take time to listen to our body and mind, and to learn from them, we will know what to do and what to avoid—giving our body and consciousness a chance for healing, transformation, and peace. When we restore peace within ourselves, we have a chance to restore peace with others.

Many people in the helping professions are challenged by

their own pain. Many doctors, nurses, social workers, psychotherapists, and teachers are suffering and do not know how to
recognize and transform their pain. They want to help relieve
other people's suffering, but they do not know how yet to take
care of their own pain and suffering. In every school of social
work, medicine, nursing, education, and law, students should
learn the practice of mindfulness and self-care as part of the cur-
riculum, not only as an intellectual pursuit, but as a part of daily
life. They would all profit personally from the study and practice
of mindfulness and be of better service to others. In a civilized
society, every school for the helping professions should teach the
practice of mindfulness.

Whenever I give retreats for health professionals, I emphasize
they must take care of themselves first before trying to help their
patients. They must learn that the way they live their personal
lives is the basis of their professional practices. When you yourself suffer deeply, when you yourself cannot communicate with
members of your own family, how can you solve the problems of
your clients and patients?

Belly Breathing to Take Care of Strong Emotions

A simple method for taking care of strong emotions is *belly breathing,* mindful breathing from the abdomen. When we are caught in
a strong emotion, such as fear or anger, we should bring our attention down to our abdomen. At times like this, to remain at the
level of the intellect is dangerous. Strong emotions are like a
storm, and it is not wise to stand in the open during a storm. Yet
our normal reaction is to stay in our head and let our feelings
overwhelm us. Instead, we should get rooted in our breathing,

focusing on the rise and fall of our abdomen, bringing our attention down to our center. When we focus on our belly and practice mindful breathing, we give all of our attention to its rise and fall. We can do this sitting or lying down. Putting a hot water bottle on the belly is also helpful. We feel the warmth of the hot water bottle and we can easily bring our gentle awareness to our stable center, allowing us to calm down.

One night, when I was in pain and could not sleep, I brought to mind the image of three cedar trees at my hermitage. With my mindful breathing, I embraced these beautiful, strong trees. I felt their freshness and stability penetrate me and I was able to overcome my painful feeling.

When you look at a tree in a windstorm, you see that the top of the tree is unstable and vulnerable. The wind can break the smaller branches at any time. But when you look down at the trunk of the tree, what you see is very different. The tree there is solid and will withstand the storm. We are like a tree. When we are upset, our head is the top of the tree being whipped around during a tempest, then we have to bring our attention down to the level of our solid trunk, our navel.

EXERCISE FOR BELLY BREATHING

When we focus on this area and begin practicing mindful breathing, we are able to calm down. We concentrate just on our breathing, on the rise and fall of our abdomen, nothing else.

1. Breathing in, I bring all my attention down to my abdomen. Breathing out, I bring all my attention down to my abdomen . . . Abdomen, Abdomen

2. Breathing in, I remain at the level of my abdomen. Breathing out, I remain at the level of my abdomen . . . Level of abdomen, Remaining

3. Breathing in, I am aware only of my abdomen rising. Breathing out, I am aware only of my abdomen falling . . . Abdomen rising, Abdomen falling

4. Breathing in, I am aware that my in breath is quick/shallow/uneven. Breathing out, I am aware that my out breath is quick/shallow/uneven . . . Breathing in, Breathing out

5. Breathing in, I am aware that my in breath is calming. Breathing out, I am aware that my out breath is slowing . . . Calming, Slowing

6. Breathing in, I am aware that my anger/despair/fear/distress is subsiding. Breathing out, I am aware that my anger/despair/fear/distress is subsiding . . . Strong emotion, Subsiding

7. Breathing in, I am aware that my anger/despair/fear/distress has passed. Breathing out, I am aware that my anger/despair/fear/distress has passed . . . Strong emotion, Passed

8. Breathing in, I am aware of my stability. Breathing out, I smile to my stability . . . Stability, Smiling

You can share this practice with your loved ones. Remind them that an emotion is just an emotion. It comes, stays for some time, and then goes away. Why should we hurt ourselves or someone else just because of a fleeting emotion? You are more than your emotions. It is important to remember this. During a crisis, remember to go immediately to your mindful breathing. Remind yourself that your painful emotion will pass. Maintain this awareness as you breathe, and keep your attention on your breath until the emotion passes. After you have succeeded in calming yourself a few times with belly breathing, you will have more confidence in yourself and in the practice.

This is a particularly important practice for parents to learn and master. Then, when your child is caught in a strong emotion, you will be able to help her. You can say, "My dear, hold my hand. Let's not get caught up in our thoughts and feelings. Let's bring our attention down to our bellies and breathe in and out. This storm will pass. Don't be afraid." Also, you can teach your child to practice belly breathing with you. By educating your child like this, you may give her the skill to save her own life later on. As an adolescent and as an adult, she will be equipped to take care of her strong emotions and navigate herself through difficult situations.

Looking Deeply at Our Strong Emotions

Once we calm our emotions using practices like belly breathing, we can look into the causes of our distress. Often we are trapped by many wrong perceptions and prejudices. We feel rejected, humiliated, ignored. We believe the other person wants to destroy us. In truth, we are afraid only because of our wrong perceptions. We practice meditation to recognize the presence of our misperceptions. We have to look deeply, to undo the knot of delusion binding our perceptions, freeing us to see that our anger arises out of ignorance and misunderstanding. When we are caught by our strong emotions, we lack lucidity and understanding.

Looking deeply, we see that the other person may be suffering and need help rather than punishment. We also see that, as long as we have no compassion for others, we suffer. Once we have understanding and compassion, we regain our happiness and peace.

MEDITATION FOR LOOKING DEEPLY AT EMOTIONS

1. Aware of my body, I breathe in. Smiling to my body, I breathe out.

2. Looking at the roots of the pain in my body, I breathe in. Smiling to the roots of pain in my body, I breathe out.

3. Aware of the contents of my mind, I breathe in. Smiling to the contents of my mind, I breathe out.

4. Looking at the roots of the pain in my mind, I breathe in. Smiling to the roots of the pain in my mind, I breathe out.

5. Looking at the roots of fear, I breathe in. Smiling to the roots of fear, I breathe out.

6. Looking at the roots of insecurity, I breathe in. Smiling to the roots of insecurity, I breathe out.

7. Looking at the roots of sadness, I breathe in. Smiling to the roots of sadness, I breathe out.

8. Looking at the roots of anger, I breathe in. Smiling at the roots of anger, I breathe out.

9. Looking at the roots of jealousy, I breathe in. Smiling at the roots of jealousy, I breathe out.

After you have taken good care of your emotions and perceptions, you might like to discuss your experiences with your family and friends. We do this to improve our relationships with those we love and to help them improve their relationships with others. This is the practice of nonviolence in action, the genuine work of transforming the world.

Restoring Body and Mind with Deep Relaxation

Stress accumulates in us every day. If you do not know how to protect yourself, stress will overcome your mind and your body. All parts of our body—our liver, heart, lungs, kidneys—send us SOS signals constantly; they are suffering, and we are often too busy to listen. We have become alienated from our own body and rarely allow it to rest or restore itself. We continue to eat, drink, and work in ways that deplete our body of its well-being. We need to learn how to listen to our bodies again. With the practice of mindfulness, we reunite our body and mind.

Deep relaxation is a wonderful mindfulness practice that lets us take care of our body. It allows us to embrace our body and give it the rest and relaxation it needs to heal itself. Breathing in and out, you become aware of each part of your body, releasing any tension you find. You take time to send love and gratitude to the different parts of your body—this can be done in only fifteen or twenty minutes.

In the beginning you may use an audiotape, but after practicing a short while you will develop your own version of Deep Relaxation Practice.

DEEP RELAXATION PRACTICE

Allowing your body to rest is very important. When your body is at ease and relaxed, your mind will also be at peace. Please take the time to do this practice often. Although the following guided relaxation may take you thirty minutes, feel free to modify it to fit your situation. You can make it shorter—just five or ten minutes. You can use it when you wake up in the morning, before going to bed in the evening, or during a short break in the middle of a busy day. You can also make it longer or more in-depth if you like. The most important thing to remember is to be fully present and to enjoy it.

- Lie down comfortably on your back on the floor or on a bed. Close your eyes. Allow your arms to rest gently on either side of your body, and let your legs relax, turning outward.

- As you breathe in and out, become aware of your whole body lying down. Feel all the areas of your body that are touching the floor or the bed you are lying on: your heels, the backs of your legs, your buttocks, your back, the backs of your hands and arms, the back of your head. With each out breath, feel yourself sink deeper and deeper into the floor, letting go of tension, letting go of worries, and not holding on to anything.

- As you breathe in, feel your abdomen rising, and as you breathe out, feel your abdomen falling. For several breaths, just notice the rise and fall of your abdomen. Now, as you breathe in, become aware of your two feet. As you breathe out, allow your feet to relax. Breathing in, send your love to your feet, and breathing out, smile to your feet. As you breathe in and out, know how wonderful it is to have two feet that allow you to walk, to run, to play sports, to dance, to drive, to do so many activities throughout the day. Send your gratitude to your two feet for always being there for you whenever you need them.

- Breathing in, become aware of your right and left legs. Breathing out, allow all the cells in your legs to relax. Breathing in, smile to your legs, and breathing out, send them your love. Appreciate whatever degree of strength and health is there in your legs. As you breathe in and out, send them your tenderness and care. Allow them to rest, sinking gently into the floor. Release any tension you may be holding in your legs.

- Breathing in, become aware of your two hands lying on the floor. Breathing out, completely relax all the muscles in your two hands, releasing any tension you may be holding in them. As you breathe in, appreciate how wonderful it is to have two hands. As you breathe out, send a smile of love to your two hands. Breathing in and out, be in touch with all the things your two hands allow you to do: to cook, to write, to drive, to hold the hand of someone else, to cradle a baby, to wash your own body, to draw, to play a musical instrument, to type, to build and fix things, to pet an animal, to hold a cup of tea. So many things are available to you because of your two hands. Just enjoy the fact that you have two hands and allow all the cells in your hands to really rest.

- Breathing in, become aware of your two arms. Breathing out, allow your arms to relax fully. As you breathe in, send your love to your arms, and as you breathe out, smile to them. Take the time to appreciate your arms and whatever strength and health is in them. Send them your gratitude for allowing you to hug someone else, to swing on a swing, to help and serve others, to work hard—cleaning the house, mowing the lawn, doing so many things throughout the day. Breathing in and out, allow your two arms to let go and rest completely on the floor. With each out breath, feel the tension leaving your arms. As you embrace your arms with your mindfulness, feel joy and ease in every part of your two arms.

• Breathing in, become aware of your shoulders. Breathing out, allow any tension in your shoulders to flow out into the floor. As you breathe in, send your love to your shoulders, and as you breathe out, smile with gratitude to them. Breathing in and out, be aware that you may have allowed a lot of tension and stress to accumulate in your shoulders. With each out breath, allow the tension to leave your shoulders, feeling them relax more and more deeply. Send them your tenderness and care, knowing that you do not want to put too much strain on them but that you want to live in a way that will allow them to be relaxed and at ease.

• Breathing in, become aware of your heart. Breathing out, allow your heart to rest. With your in breath, send your love to your heart. With your out breath, smile to your heart. As you breathe in and out, get in touch with how wonderful it is to have a heart still beating in your chest. Your heart allows your life to be possible, and it is always there for you, every minute, every day. It never takes a break. Your heart has been beating continuously since you were a four-week-old fetus in your mother's womb. It is a marvelous organ that allows you to do everything you do throughout the day. Breathe in and know that your heart also loves you. Breathe out and commit to live in a way that will help your heart to function well. With each out breath, feel your heart relaxing more and more. Allow each cell in your heart to smile with ease and joy.

- Breathing in, become aware of your stomach and intestines. Breathing out, allow your stomach and intestines to relax. As you breathe in, send them your love and gratitude. As you breathe out, smile tenderly to them. Breathing in and out, know how essential these organs are to your health. Give them the chance to rest deeply. Each day they digest and assimilate the food you eat, giving you energy and strength. They need you to take the time to recognize and appreciate them. As you breathe in, feel your stomach and intestines relaxing and releasing all tension. As you breathe out, enjoy the fact that you have a healthy stomach and intestines.

- Breathing in, become aware of your eyes. Breathing out, allow your eyes and the muscles around your eyes to relax. Breathing in, smile to your eyes, and breathing out, send them your love. Allow your eyes to rest and roll back into your head. As you breathe in and out, know how precious your two eyes are. They allow you to look into the eyes of someone you love, to see a beautiful sunset, to read and write, to move around with ease, to see a bird flying in the sky, to watch a movie—so many things are possible because of your two eyes. Take the time to appreciate the gift of sight, and allow your eyes to rest deeply. You can gently raise your eyebrows to help release any tension you may be holding around your eyes.

· Here you can continue to relax other areas of your body, using the same pattern.

· Now, if there is a place in your body that is sick or in pain, take this time to become aware of it and send it your love. Breathing in, allow this area to rest, and breathing out, smile to it with great tenderness and affection. Be aware that there are other parts of your body that are still strong and healthy. Allow these strong parts of your body to send their strength and energy to the weak or sick area. Feel the support, energy, and love of the rest of your body penetrating the weak area, soothing and healing it. Breathe in and affirm your own capacity to heal, breathe out and let go of the worry or fear you may be holding in your body. Breathing in and out, smile with love and confidence to the area of your body that is not well.

· When you feel a great deal of pain and sickness in your body, you may also call on your ancestors to support you. You know that all your ancestors are present in every cell of your body. Identify one of your ancestors who was strong and healthy. Breathing in, call on the strength and vitality of your ancestor to support you. Breathing out, you will feel his or her energy and presence in you, helping you to restore your strength and well-being.

· Breathing in, become aware of the whole of your body lying down. Breathing out, enjoy the sensation of your whole body lying down, very relaxed and calm. Smile to your whole body as you breathe in, and send your love and compassion to your whole body as you breathe out. Feel all the cells in your whole body smiling joyfully with you. Feel gratitude for all the cells in your whole body.

- If you are guiding other people, especially children, and if you are comfortable doing so, you can sing a relaxing song or lullaby.

- To end, bring your awareness back to the gentle rise and fall of your abdomen. Slowly stretch your body and open your eyes. Take your time to sit up slowly and peacefully. Now you can carry the energy of calm, mindfulness, and peace you have generated into your next activity and throughout the day.

CHAPTER THREE

PEACE BEGINS WITH US

TAKING YOUR PRACTICE INTO THE WORLD

In 1968, during the height of the Vietnam War, my student Sister Chan Khong was doing reconstruction work in Thao Diên. In this relatively peaceful village, we had sponsored many projects to help peasants improve their livelihoods. One day as Sister Chan Khong arrived at the village, she was shocked to see it had been invaded by a platoon of American soldiers carrying grenades and machine guns. They looked anxious and scared, as if at any time they might start shooting. At that moment, the Sister remembered the reports in all the Vietnamese papers about My Lai, where American soldiers had killed an entire village of mostly women, children, and elderly people. She realized then that if just one person in the village started to scream or behave in an agitated way, it could ignite the fear in the hearts of the American soldiers, causing them to open fire on everyone, just as in My Lai.

Sister Chan Khong brought her awareness to her breath and

calmed herself so that she could see what to do and what not to do in this dangerous situation. Looking at the faces of the American soldiers, she could see how young they were, the same age as many of her own students at the university. She could see they were overwhelmed with fear.

Sister Chan Khong slowly approached one of the soldiers and, using her limited English, politely asked, "What do you want to search for? What can I do to help you?" The young American was surprised to hear someone speak English to him. As he looked at the shy young woman standing before him, he met her eyes and saw she was sincerely trying to help. He said, "We want to search for the Communists." Sister Chan Khong replied, "There are no Communists in this village." She continued, "Four days ago a troop of guerrillas came to the village. They wanted to kill the chief of the village and burn his house. But the villagers begged them not to because all houses here are made from palm leaves, and if you burn his house you will burn all our houses. We asked the gunmen, please, do not kill this man—he is a good person. If you kill him the Saigon Government will send another man who could be terrible to us."

The young soldier listened to Sister Chan Khong and then called to the officer in charge, who came over and asked her similar questions. The Sister explained again that there were no Communists in the village. Half an hour later, the whole platoon of Americans withdrew. Bloodshed was avoided and peace was restored thanks to the mindfulness and the calmness of a young lady who knew how to breathe, how to look deeply, and how to communicate compassionately with the soldiers.

The war stops and starts with you and with me. Every morning when you open your eyes, the potential for violence and war begins. So every morning, when you open your eyes, please, water the seeds of compassion and nonviolence. Try selecting a mindfulness practice that helps you transform your own internal conflicts. Let peace begin with you.

When we practice mindfulness in our daily life, we cultivate the foundation of peace, sowing seeds of understanding in ourselves and others.

We are all eager to prevent and to end war. Many of us want to do something, but we often feel hopeless and helpless. Please do not allow these feelings to overwhelm you; they are of no benefit to you or the world. You can help make peace, but just making declarations opposing war is not enough. We may shout over and over again, "Violence is inhuman and destructive," but shouting alone will not end war. Every mindful step we make and every mindful breath we take will establish peace in the present moment and prevent war in the future.

If we transform our individual consciousness, we begin the process of changing the collective consciousness. Transforming the world's consciousness is not possible without personal change. The collective is made of the individual, and the individual is made of the collective, and each and every individual has a direct effect on the collective consciousness.

Our Only Weapon Is Love

One day in 1965, while I was a monk at the Truc Lam Monastery in Saigon, my monastic student Brother Nhat Tri was walking in the streets of the city. An American military truck passed by, and an American soldier standing on the back of the truck spit on his head. Brother Nhat Tri came to me and cried because he felt so humiliated. I told him the American soldier had probably heard a lot of propaganda that Buddhist monks and nuns were Communists in disguise. Therefore, when the soldier saw Brother Nhat Tri, he showed his hatred by spitting on him. The American GI was a victim of misperception and ignorance. I said, "Brother, you should not hate him. If you hate him, it means you have not yet understood." In such awful situations, many young people wanted to forsake their practice of nonviolence and join the National Liberation Front, picking up a gun in order to fight the Americans. I held Brother Nhat Tri in my arms for a long time, saying, "My child, we are not born to hold a gun, we are born to love. Love is the only weapon we carry." These words helped him reconnect to his original purpose, and he stayed to continue his social work.

The world is full of discrimination, violence, and hatred. If we allow ourselves to be caught by these negative energies, we cannot help each other or our planet. Instead, we must cultivate freedom, solidity, and understanding. You do not have to be a monk or a nun to practice like this. You need only the willingness to open your heart to the goodness within you, your Buddha nature, the Mind of Love.

Writing a Love Letter

People often think, If only I had the chance to express my frustration and pain, I would feel better. Yet many of us have tried this in the past, and it has not helped. We have vented our frustration and anger, our pain and complaints many times, and still we feel unsatisfied. There is a better alternative.

When you have practiced transforming your own inner pain, you can begin to learn how to express yourself in a way in which the other person can listen, so that he or she can really hear what you have to say. If we only insult or condemn, our speech will be of no use. With mindfulness, we practice to be honest and to be skillful at the same time. Many people are capable of writing a letter of protest, a letter of dissatisfaction or a complaint, but not many of us are capable of writing a love letter. Expressing yourself with love is an art. When you have understanding and compassion, you will succeed in expressing your concerns to the other person. When you are angry, blaming, and punishing in tone, you will not succeed. You will only make the gulf between you wider. You must protest acting with the Mind of Love. When you are able to give rise to the Mind of Love, you are in a good position to begin writing your love letter. Your letter will reflect your calm, your clarity, and your compassion, and the other person will be able to receive what you want to say.

Further Training in Compassion and Peace Work

I have a friend who lives in central Europe and is an environmental activist. He is very angry. He is not happy with his wife, parents, friends, or society. He pollutes his body and mind with nicotine, alcohol, and negative judgments about other people.

He does not know how to make peace within. He is a militant in the protection of the environment but not in the protection of himself. I doubt very much that he will succeed in helping the environment because he tries to defend the planet with his anger, violence, and self-pollution. This is not the way to protect nature.

Whenever we hold retreats for environmentalists at Plum Village, we say, "Dear friends, please take care of yourself if you want to protect the environment. The very well-being of the planet depends on the way you handle your body, your feelings, your perceptions, and your consciousness. In the same way, the well-being of your body and mind depends on the well-being of the planet. If you cannot deal with the problem of pollution and violence within you, how can you deal with the problem of pollution and violence outside of you, in nature?" In fact, we say this same thing to all the professionals who come to Plum Village.

Engaged peace workers need to be strong, stable, and genuinely peaceful. Inner balance is crucial for peace work. If we lose our own mindfulness, we cannot be helpful. We should not try to help others in an effort to escape our own sorrow, despair, or inner conflict. If you are not peaceful and solid enough inside yourself, your contributions will not be useful. We must first practice mindfulness and grow compassion in ourselves, so that peace and harmony are in us, before we can work effectively for social change.

Of course, you do not have to wait until you achieve perfect peace and harmony before you engage in social action. Every time we are able to restore even a small amount of peace within

ourselves, we already have a positive effect on our family and society. Know your limits and nourish yourself with the practice of
mindfulness, then you will find an inner balance.

We must sustain our spiritual practice to avoid burnout. The
best way to do this is in the context of a community of practice,
which in Buddhism we call *sangha*. I recommend to friends who
are engaged in helping others to set aside one day a week to practice together with a sangha. During the other six days, when
working, try always to practice mindful breathing and mindful
walking and to maintain peace and stability. Alone we will lose
our ability to help. We must act together.

Compassion Leads to Happiness

It is easy to tell how happy someone is by observing how compassionate she is toward others. Life is precious. Those who recognize this preciousness and offer peace and protection to other
living beings find peace and protection available to themselves. If
we are motivated to protect the lives of all animals, even the
smallest insect, then we will never want to take human life. With
compassion, you see others as yourself. You see how we all inter-
are. So many people feel completely cut off from life and its
many forms. We all need to find the conditions to develop our
compassion.

Fifteen years ago, a business manager from the United States
came to Plum Village to visit me. His conscience was troubled because he was the head of a firm that designed atomic bombs. I listened as he expressed his concerns. I knew if I advised him to quit
his job, another person would only replace him. If he were to

quit, he might help himself, but he would not help his company, society, or country. I urged him to remain the director of his firm, to bring mindfulness into his daily work, and to use his position to communicate his concerns and doubts about the production of atomic bombs.

In the Sutra on Happiness, the Buddha says it is a great fortune to have an occupation that allows us to be happy, to help others, and to generate compassion and understanding in this world. Those in the helping professions have occupations that give them this wonderful opportunity. Yet many social workers, physicians, and therapists work in a way that does not cultivate their compassion, instead doing their job only to earn money. If the bomb designer practices and does his work with mindfulness, his job can still nourish his compassion and in some way allow him to help others. He can still influence his government and fellow citizens by bringing greater awareness to the situation. He can give the whole nation an opportunity to question the necessity of bomb production.

Many people who are wealthy, powerful, and important in business, politics, and entertainment are not happy. They are seeking empty things—wealth, fame, power, sex—and in the process they are destroying themselves and those around them. In Plum Village, we have organized retreats for businesspeople. We see that they have many problems and suffer just as others do, sometimes even more. We see that their wealth allows them to live in comfortable conditions, yet they still suffer a great deal.

Some businesspeople, even those who have persuaded themselves that their work is very important, feel empty in their occupation. They provide employment to many people in their factories, newspapers, insurance firms, and supermarket chains, yet their financial success is an empty happiness because it is not motivated by understanding or compassion. Caught up in their small world of profit and loss, they are unaware of the suffering and poverty in the world. When we are not in touch with this larger reality, we will lack the compassion we need to nourish and guide us to happiness.

Once you begin to realize your interconnectedness with others, your interbeing, you begin to see how your actions affect you and all other life. You begin to question your way of living, to look with new eyes at the quality of your relationships and the way you work. You begin to see, "I have to earn a living, yes, but I want to earn a living mindfully. I want to try to select a vocation not harmful to others and to the natural world, one that does not misuse resources."

Entire companies can also adopt this way of thinking. Companies have the right to pursue economic growth, but not at the expense of other life. They should respect the life and integrity of people, animals, plants, and minerals. Do not invest your time or money in companies that deprive others of their lives, that operate in a way that exploits people or animals, and destroys nature.

Businesspeople who visit Plum Village often find that getting in touch with the suffering of others and cultivating understanding brings them happiness. They practice like Anathapindika, a successful businessman who lived at the time of the Buddha, who with the practice of mindfulness throughout his life did everything he could to help the poor and sick people in his homeland.

Finding True Refuge in Practice

Many people who suffer in their personal lives seek relief by taking refuge in their work. I know a doctor in California who works very hard taking care of his patients. After his office closes, he stays on for hours and studies his patients' files because he does not want to go home. His wife is used to this, because they are not a happy couple. It is more comfortable for him to stay in his office and study. He tells himself, "This is a good thing I am doing, I am a good doctor, I have to stay in the office and work, to understand my patients' problems better." He takes refuge in this use of his time to give his life more meaning. Deep down he knows, but does not want to accept, that he is taking refuge in his work to avoid confronting the real problem, his marriage. In our society, it is very common for people to take refuge in their work and deny their unhappiness.

Many others take refuge in drugs and alcohol. They want to forget, they want to dull the pain within them. When they get drunk or high, they forget everything, but only for a few hours. When they wake up from this self-anesthesia, they realize that nothing has changed. Still, they have evaded reality for two or three hours, and since they do not know any other way out, again they resort to drugs or alcohol. Doing so, they violate their bodies and minds, and create suffering for themselves and the people around them. This is no solution at all.

In modern society, many of us also take refuge in consumption. When we do not feel good about ourselves, when we feel empty or depressed, we turn to the refrigerator or go to the shopping mall in order to fill the void and forget our suffering. We take refuge in the act of eating, drinking, or shopping. We are trying to fill the emptiness inside because we do not know what to take refuge in. We seek distraction by feeding our senses.

Many people also take refuge in television. We allow ourselves to be occupied by the program, becoming the television. Some programs are nourishing and educational, but most are not. They are like junk food that contains only noise and violence. Even though ingesting these programs does not make us feel good, we still leave the TV on to evade the real issues in our lives. We cannot turn it off, because when we do, we have to go back to ourselves, and this is uncomfortable. We watch television endlessly to avoid the program that is running inside us—an ongoing program of confusion, conflict, and despair. We turn away from our own suffering because we lack the confidence to deal with the issues that really matter.

We need to break the habit of running away from ourselves. We want peace, we want security, joy, and happiness, but we do not know how to get these things. Taking refuge in the practice of mindfulness is our path. It gives us confidence to overcome our difficulties. We can take refuge in our mindful breathing, in our mindful steps. Then we will have peace and be available for the wonders of life; we will be truly present for our children, our families, and our society.

A True Peace Walk

Many people like to participate in walks for peace. In 1981, on the day the United Nations decided whether to pass a resolution on disarmament, a huge march was organized in New York City. Half a million people walked together for peace. When some of my friends invited me to join the march, I agreed to participate only if I could walk in the style of walking meditation. My friends assured me that this was possible, a group of fifty people joined with me, and we walked together to support this practice.

We were a multinational, multicultural group representing many spiritual traditions. Holding a banner that read, "Reverence for Life," we walked mindfully down the streets of Manhattan. Groups of young people around us were marching quickly, almost running, and shouting slogans like "Disarmament now! Down with nuclear weapons!" Our group did not say anything; we just walked slowly and peacefully. We learned later that, because of our way of walking, we slowed 300,000 people behind us. Throughout the long walk, there were groups behind us shouting, "Can't you walk faster?" trying to pass us. When they went by us, they would look back in frustration at this cluster of people who were moving so slowly. But then a curious thing happened. As they watched us, they changed their attitude, quieted down, and began to walk more slowly themselves. It became a true peace walk. People still remember this walk because of the small group in the "March for Peace" who actually practiced peace with every step they took.

THERE IS NO walk for peace; peace must be the walk. You do not need to finish a walk to have peace. The practice is simply to embody peace during the walk. The means are the ends. If you are fond of walking for peace, you should turn your walk into the practice of peace. This is the way to touch the hearts of people. What is important is not the number of miles you walk but the quality of each step you take. Peace always begins with you. When you walk mindfully, people will be touched by you. If there is a rally or demonstration for peace, please organize, please participate in such a way that peace is possible, that the event itself is peace.

True Refuge

We need to have enough confidence, faith, and courage to call our actions by their true names. We should ask ourselves, Are we engaging in a lifestyle that touches the beauty and goodness within and around us, and leads us in the direction of compassion and understanding? Or are we simply seeking to escape from ourselves?

True refuge is something that opens the door of transformation and healing to us. We need to learn how to take refuge. Taking refuge is not an act of escape. It is an act of protection and inclusiveness. If what we now take refuge in—work, food, material comfort, television—cuts us off from our own feelings, our family, and our society, it is not really a place of refuge. If our lifestyle numbs us to the reality of our suffering and that of others, we are moving in the wrong direction. We are isolating ourselves, and we are committing violence in the form of exclusion. Running after sensual distraction and pleasure, we think we can escape our suffering and find true happiness, but happiness does not lie in the direction of sensual pleasure. Happiness lies in finding inner peace.

Psychologists who study happiness have found that truly happy people are fully present in the moment. They do not focus on threats or negative possibilities but search constantly for ways to make everyone benefit in difficult situations. Happy people work with and help others. For them happiness is not a goal to be achieved but a reality in their everyday life.

Taking Time to Live

When I was young, life in Vietnam was quite different from the way it is now. We did not have many machines, and we were more relaxed in our daily life. If you wanted to organize a birthday party, a poetry reading, or the anniversary of a family member's death, the reception would take all day long, not only a few hours. You could arrive at any time, and the whole day was reserved for the event. You did not need to have a car or a bike—you just walked. If you lived far away, you started out the day before and spent the night at a friend's house along the way. No matter what time you arrived, you were welcomed and served food. When four people came, they were served together at a table. If you were the fifth, you waited until three others came so you could eat together with them. You could talk, recite poetry, and sing together, and you could stay on or leave any time you wanted.

In today's world, we do not have such luxury. We do have more money and more material comfort, but we are not really happier because we simply do not have time to enjoy each other.

Years ago in Vietnam, people used to take a small boat out into a lotus pond and put some tea leaves into an open lotus flower. The flower would close in the evening and perfume the tea during the night. In the early morning, when the dew was still on the leaves, you would return with your friends to collect the tea. On your boat was everything you needed: fresh water, a stove to heat it, teacups, and a teapot. Then, in the beautiful light of the morning, you prepared the tea right there, enjoying the whole morning, drinking tea on the lotus pond. Nowadays you may have a lotus pond, but you do not have the time to look at it, let alone enjoy it in that way.

A tea meditation is a remnant of these times when we used to spend two or three hours drinking a cup of tea. In Plum Village, we are fortunate to have tea ceremonies several times a month. We come together to enjoy a cup of tea, a cookie, and the company of others for about an hour and a half. In a serene, affectionate, and informal atmosphere, we share poems, songs, and stories. We need only two minutes to drink a cup of tea, but in taking time to be with others, we nourish mutual understanding and happiness.

In Vietnam in past years, when someone noticed the cherry tree in his backyard was about to bloom, he would invite over relatives and friends, carefully writing out personal invitations to come celebrate the blossoms' opening. The whole family helped to prepare the event, baking wheat germ cookies and arranging everything nicely. With events like this, we took every opportunity to enjoy life, and to be together with friends, drinking tea, singing, and reciting poetry.

Then, if the weather turned cold and the cherry tree was not going to blossom on time, people would gather to play a drum at the foot of the tree, helping to stimulate it to blossom. Today these festivities are thought of as uneconomical because time is money. For us, as practitioners of mindfulness, time should be much more precious than money. Time is life; we should use our time in order to live with peace, joy, and freedom.

Mindfulness Nurtures a Simple Lifestyle

As you grow in mindfulness, you take back your life. You begin to see how much time we lose in empty consumption. When we are consuming, we are also being consumed—we have become the objects of other people's consumption. The Buddha said, "Dear friends, you are being eaten by form and by feelings. You are being consumed."

We make ourselves into merchandise for other people. We want to be alluring and sought after, so we buy new clothes or a new perfume. We work out at the gym to make ourselves more attractive and turn ourselves into objects of desire for other people, other consumers. Although we must take care of ourselves, we do many of these things because we believe this kind of consumption will bring happiness. We should look more deeply to see that this empty consumption brings us no happiness, only suffering.

The objects of our consumption are always changing. And our desires for the objects we consume are always changing from moment to moment. We are always running after something new. We may be infatuated with what we buy for a while, but soon we throw it away and buy something else. When I first came to live in France, our sangha bought a little car, a secondhand Peugeot. We went all over Europe in it, using the car to transport not only people but sand, bricks, tools, books, food, and many other materials. We used it for all our needs and kept it for many years.

When our car was old and could not be used anymore, we had a difficult time letting it go. We were attached to our little Peugeot, because we and the car had gone through so much together. It had survived breakdowns, numerous accidents, and untold repairs. My friends in the sangha and I were sad the night we had to abandon it. I even wrote a poem in remembrance of it.

These days, people rarely develop a connection to the things they buy, they just desire to possess the newest thing. Manufacturers know this. It is not by accident that merchandise in modern times is not created to last. If these products were to last a long time, there would be fewer profits for the manufacturers, who depend on us to constantly buy the new, new thing.

We feel we never have enough because we are caught up in the philosophy that too much is never enough. We have not given ourselves the opportunity to look deeply into our way of consuming. However, when we take the time to live mindfully, we will discover that living a simple life and consuming less are the true conditions for happiness.

The Buddha taught that we should be satisfied with the basic conditions of life and know when we have enough. The way monks and nuns lived in the time of the Buddha is a vivid example of this practice. They had no more than three robes and a bowl. They understood that material possessions do not bring true happiness. We live a simple lifestyle in order to be happy. The practice of living simply has many advantages: when you are no longer running after possessions, you need less money and can afford to work less. You have more time to do things that are meaningful and enjoyable.

There is a Confucian saying that expresses this well: "If you know what is enough, then you will have enough. But if you wait until you have enough, you will never have enough."

A Civilized Culture

The words *civilization* and *civilized* share similar meanings. *Civilized* is the opposite of *violent*, signifying beauty, gentleness, and peace. A civilized society and culture are the fruit of our practice; harmony and compassion are their hallmarks. Mindfulness practice reflects the notion of culture: we cultivate freedom, responsibility, and understanding, and reap their fruits. Peace, like sunflowers, must be cultivated so it can grow. In the beginning, all we have is soil, and then we have to plow the earth and sow the seeds. If we water the soil and take good care of the plants, in a few months we will have beautiful sunflowers. The same is true of peace.

As civilized practitioners of mindfulness, we must learn to recognize when we are living at the expense of other living beings—humans, animals, plants, the living soil, water, and air of our planet—and when we are committing violence by our unmindful way of living, consuming, and producing. The practice of mindful living helps us stop, to see what we are doing and where we are headed. When we allow ourselves the time to look deeply, we give understanding and compassion a chance to grow in our hearts, and we can then act on our insights.

The Five Mindfulness Trainings

In this book on nonviolence, I often refer to the Five Mindfulness Trainings. The Buddha likened the body to a water pitcher, holding and dispensing what we put into it. He advised us to use mindfulness as a guardian of our consciousness and our body. The Mindfulness Trainings help us learn to exercise self-protection. They present clear, practical ways to implement the spirit of peace in our daily lives. They are our tools for peace.

We tend to think that the violence we suffer comes only from others, from outside ourselves, but this is not correct. We inflict violence upon our own body and consciousness by our way of eating, drinking, or working. When we consume, read, or view certain products, we inflict violence on ourselves. Our consciousness as well as our body can be victim to mindless consumption. When we consume something that is not healthy for our body, we are not loving ourselves, we are violating ourselves. Television programs, magazines, films, or conversations that contain violence and craving promote inner conflict. We often live our daily life in forgetfulness, allowing consumption to intoxicate us and our children. With the Mindfulness Trainings we can learn to detect these elements when they manifest and protect ourselves from them.

The Five Mindfulness Trainings originated many years ago as a gift of the Buddha. They are worded in such a way that everyone can apply them, regardless of spiritual tradition or cultural background.

All of these trainings help keep us conscious of our thoughts and actions. They help us cultivate nonviolent thoughts and nonviolent actions. The Buddha said that we cannot only talk about doing what is beneficial, we have to put it into practice. By practicing these trainings, we gain more awareness of the suffering caused by the violence in our thoughts, words, and actions.

THE FIVE MINDFULNESS TRAININGS

The First Mindfulness Training: *Reverence for Life*

Aware of the suffering caused by the destruction of life, I vow to cultivate compassion and learn ways to protect the lives of people, animals, plants, and minerals. I am determined not to kill, not to let others kill, and not to condone any act of killing in the world, in my thinking, or in my way of life.

The Second Mindfulness Training: *Generosity*

Aware of the suffering caused by exploitation, social injustice, stealing, and oppression, I vow to cultivate loving-kindness and learn ways to work for the well-being of people, animals, plants, and minerals. I vow to practice generosity by sharing my time, energy, and material resources with those who are in real need. I am determined not to steal and not to possess anything that should belong to others. I will respect the property of others, but I will prevent others from profiting from human suffering or the suffering of other species on earth.

The Third Mindfulness Training: *Sexual Responsibility*

Aware of the suffering caused by sexual misconduct, I vow to cultivate responsibility and learn ways to protect the safety and integrity of individuals, couples, families, and society. I am determined not to engage in sexual relations without love and a long-term commitment. To preserve the happiness of others, and myself, I am determined to respect my commitments and the commitments of others. I will do everything in my power to protect children from sexual abuse and to protect couples and families from being broken by sexual misconduct.

The Fourth Mindfulness Training:
Deep Listening and Loving Speech

Aware of the suffering caused by the inability to listen to others and unmindful speech, I vow to cultivate deep listening and loving speech in order to bring joy and happiness to others and relieve others of their suffering. Knowing that words can create happiness or suffering, I vow to learn to speak truthfully with words that inspire self-confidence, joy, and hope. I am determined not to spread news that I do not know to be certain, and not to criticize or condemn things of which I am not sure. I will refrain from uttering words that can cause division or discord, or that can cause the family or the community to break. I will make all efforts to reconcile and resolve all conflicts, however small.

The Fifth Mindfulness Training: *Mindful Consumption*

Aware of the suffering caused by unmindful consumption, I vow to cultivate good health, both physical and mental, for myself, my family, and my society by practicing mindful eating, drinking, and consuming. I vow to ingest only items that preserve peace, well-being, and joy in my body, in my consciousness, and in the collective body and consciousness of my family and society. I understand that a proper diet is crucial for self-transformation and for the transformation of society. I am determined not to use alcohol or any other intoxicant, or to ingest food or other items that contain toxins, such as certain TV programs, magazines, books, films, and conversations. I am aware that to damage my body or my consciousness with these poisons is to betray my ancestors, my parents, my society, and future generations. I will work to transform violence, fear, anger, and confusion in myself and in society by practicing mindful eating for myself and for society.

On the basis of this awareness, we are then motivated to relieve suffering and to foster peace in ourselves and others.

In English, we have the verb *to be*. The Mindfulness Trainings show us the reality of how to *inter-be*. As humans we cannot just be. We need other people. We need other animals, and we need our beautiful planet. The Five Mindfulness Trainings help us protect ourselves from being consumed as we protect the lives of other humans and of animals, plants, and minerals of the living soil. Simple living and compassion are manifestations of these trainings and also the basic tenets of interbeing.

When we practice one training, we are practicing the other trainings as well. They are all interrelated. When we practice respecting life (the First Mindfulness Training), we are more careful of what and of how we consume (the Fifth Mindfulness Training), and we do this to protect the lives of humans, animals, plants, and minerals. We learn to spend our time and resources wisely (the Second Mindfulness Training), buying only what we need and investing only in companies that respect life and our mother Earth.

The trainings are interrelated because the practice of mindfulness is interwoven into all aspects of our life. We ourselves are interrelated—any action we do has an effect on everything around us. In modern times, it is easy to see that "no man is an island." It is not really possible "to be"; it is only possible to "inter-be."

When we eat mindfully, we maintain awareness of all the living beings whose existence and hard work have contributed to the food in front of us. This awareness of our interdependence with other beings helps us maintain compassion in our heart. To emphasize this interdependence, the Buddha told a parable called "The Son's Flesh," about a young couple who wanted to live in another country. To do so, they had to cross a dangerous, wide desert. The young couple brought their little boy along, but halfway through the desert they ran out of food. They knew that they were going to die. After much debate they decided to kill their little son and eat his flesh. They killed the child, ate one piece of his flesh, and preserved the rest on their shoulders for the sun to dry. They suffered tremendously. Every time they ate a piece of their son's flesh, they would cry out in despair, "Where are you, our sweet boy? Where are you, our sweet boy?" They beat their chests and pulled their hair. Eventually, they crossed the desert and entered the other land.

After telling this story to his monks, the Buddha asked, "Dear friends, do you think the couple enjoyed eating the flesh of their son?" And the monks replied, "No, how could anyone enjoy eating the flesh of their own son?" To which the Buddha said, "If we do not consume mindfully, it is as if we were eating the flesh of our own son or daughter."

When we drink alcohol and eat meat, because these substances are made from the suffering of other people and beings and of our mother Earth, it is as if we are eating our own flesh and blood. When we consider the drinking of alcohol through the Fifth Mindfulness Training, we see that the production of alcohol creates suffering. Drinking alcohol causes disease in the body and the mind, and leads to many deaths in car accidents. Alcohol production requires large amounts of grain that could be used to feed the starving people of the world. Alcohol is directly related to the suffering of children. For instance, to make one glass of rice wine takes a whole basket of rice. Every day 40,000 children die in the world for lack of food. We who overeat in the West, who are feeding grains to animals to make meat, are eating the flesh of these children.

All of us, including children, have the capacity to see the suffering of animals used for food. The way we create food is very violent. It destroys mother Earth. It causes pollution of the earth and water. It destroys forests, which are cleared for agriculture, forests which are the lungs of the Earth, providing us all with oxygen. It destroys the happiness and lives of our fellow creatures. When we practice mindful eating, we become aware that we are eating our mother, our father, and our children. We are consuming the Earth.

That is why the Buddha recommended that we look at how

and what we consume, so that we can stop the suffering of the Earth and all species around us, as well as the suffering that we cause ourselves as a result. Food can be delicious without using the flesh of animals. Once we are aware, we have the chance to stop the killing of animals and begin moving in the direction of vegetarian living.

If the overdeveloped countries in the West were to reduce their consumption of meat and alcohol by 30 percent, they would solve the problem of hunger in the world. As we practice the Mindfulness Trainings, our way of living comes to nurture our awareness of what we are doing in our daily life and brings us liberating insights. The trainings help us to live a simpler, healthier, more compassionate lifestyle for the benefit of all beings.

Preserving Our Heritage by Mindful Consumption: The Four Kinds of Food

In the "Sutra on the Son's Flesh," the Buddha also taught that there are four kinds of food that we consume. The first kind is called edible food, which is what we take into our body. We practice mindful consumption of edible foods to avoid doing violence to our body. Our body has been handed down to us by many generations, and we have no right to destroy it by the way we eat and drink. When we consume toxins like drugs or alcohol, we are unkind to our ancestors, our children, and to their children because we are destroying what we received from our ancestors and will pass on to future generations. People tend to think, "This is my body; I can do anything I want to it because it belongs to me." This is a wrong view, our body does not belong to us alone; it belongs to our ancestors, family, and children as well. Your body is the continuation of your father, mother, and ancestors. You have to take good care of it so you can transmit your best to your children and your grandchildren, your partner and community.

Edible Food: The First Food

Humans can never be completely nonviolent, but we can certainly move in this direction. As we continue to practice, we can reduce the amount of violence in various aspects of our life, like the food we eat. The degree to which we are civilized can be seen in the amount of understanding, compassion, and nonviolence we have in producing and consuming food.

The same is true with being perfectly vegetarian. You cannot be a perfect vegetarian, because when you cook or boil vegetables, you are killing microorganisms. Nevertheless, we need to eat to survive. The way we procure and eat our food should be humane.

Many people in the food industry are interested only in making money. They are not motivated by understanding or compassion. They indiscriminately use large amounts of chemical fertilizer and pesticides, in the process destroying the environment, harming other humans, and killing other species. This is not civilized behavior. Our food can be produced and distributed in a sensitive, nonviolent way that does not harm us or other species.

Sense Impressions: The Second Food

The second type of food is sense impressions. We are constantly consuming with our eyes, nose, tongue, ears, body, and with our mind consciousness. It is our responsibility to consume sense impressions mindfully so as not to do violence to our consciousness. When you read a novel or a newspaper, you are consuming; when you listen to music or a conversation, you are consuming; when you drive through the city and see and hear advertisements, these sense impressions are all objects of your consumption.

Sense impressions can be toxic if we are not mindful of them. Music can feed your seeds of craving, sorrow, and violence. The article you read can feed the energy of fear or anger in you. A conversation can create despair and hatred in you. Sights, sounds, ideas—they all belong to this second category of food. We have to be very mindful in consuming these things or they will make us angrier and angrier every day. Can someone in your family embody the practice of mindful consumption? Do your child's teachers and schools understand that happiness and peace depend on the way we protect senses?

When a typical child in America finishes elementary school, she has watched about 100,000 acts of violence and 8,000 murders on television. This is too much. This means we and our children are consuming thoughts of violence, hatred, craving, and despair every day. Without mindful consumption, we will continue to accumulate the toxins of violence and craving in our consciousness, and our family and society will suffer the consequences.

The Buddha advised us to be mindful, to avoid things that can bring such toxins into our consciousness. He used as an example the story of a cow with skin disease. The skin disease on the cow is so serious that she does not seem to have any skin at all. Without skin to protect her, she is vulnerable wherever she goes. When the cow is close to a tree, all the tiny living beings in the tree come out and suck the blood on the body of the cow. When the cow is close to an ancient wall, all the tiny living beings inside the wall come out and attach to the cow. The cow has no means of self-protection. If we do not practice mindful consumption, we too will be like cows without skin, and the toxins of violence, despair, and craving will continue to penetrate into us and weaken us.

That is why it is very important to wake up and to reject the kind of production and consumption that is destroying us, our nation, our young people. Every one of us has to practice looking deeply into our situation and see where and how we are contributing to violence every day.

On cigarette packages you can now read a warning that smoking is dangerous to our health. This is a major achievement in the practice of mindfulness. It is our collective awareness manifested in legislative action. Twenty years ago, nonsmoking airline flights were only a dream, and people suffered from cigarette smoke while flying. Now all of us can enjoy a smoke-free flight. This is a victory of mindfulness. Without the work of many people, we could not have this freedom. We have to strengthen our efforts to protect ourselves. The number of people who die from drunk driving and alcohol abuse is enormous. We must strictly forbid the sale of alcohol to minors. And we should have a sentence on every bottle of alcohol: "Warning: Drinking alcohol is hazardous to your health. It can kill you and lead you to kill others."

I believe we should also make our own labels to put on our television sets: "Warning: Watching TV can be dangerous." We must be vigilant in protecting ourselves from TV's negative influences. Television is like a plug-in drug. If you are a parent or an educator, you in particular cannot ignore this issue because it directly affects the peace and stability of your children.

In the everyday world, we are continually bombarded by images and sounds that stimulate our animal nature. This situation causes many people to become physically sick and mentally ill, even to the point of such depravity as molesting children and other sexual misconduct that destroys individuals and families. For our protection and that of our children, we should abstain from consuming these products that are toxic to our well-being. At a practice center, our Buddha nature is touched every day. Everything we see, hear, smell, taste, or touch can foster our understanding and compassion rather than harm us. A community can help us practice these Mindfulness Trainings and take responsibility as consumers.

Mindful Intentions: The Third Food

The third source of food is our volition, which means our intention, our deepest desire. Our volition is what motivates us to live the way we do. If we are living in a way that engenders violence, we have to ask ourselves if it has something to do with our desire for sensual pleasure, fame, wealth, or power. If we desire to serve humanity, to relieve the suffering of others, to bring about well-being and peace, what is actually driving us, our altruistic or our animal desires?

To illustrate the third kind of food, volition, the Buddha offers us the image of a two strong men who are pulling a young person into a pit of burning charcoal. The strong men are the force of our wrong desires, which push us into the place of great suffering. When we guard ourselves with mindfulness and compassion, we can resist, and our volition will take us in the direction of peace.

As a bodhisattva in training, you are motivated by the deep desire for both yourself and others to be free from suffering and afflictions. Yet many well-intentioned people have deviated from their true desires to help humanity and have been caught in fame, pleasure, wealth, and power. If we go on the path of excess consumption and exploitation, this is the wrong direction and will bring a lot of unhappiness to ourselves and other people. This is why it is important to identify and remember the true nature of our deepest desire. We want to get back on the right path. Our nations, too, need to engage in this sort of deep reflection on their collective purpose and desire.

Sometimes we think we are acting for the cause of peace, love, and understanding, but in fact we may be working for our own fame, profit, and power. Often our selfish desires remain hidden because we think we are serving the cause of humanity. We can easily fool ourselves, but with deep reflection we will see the truth. We have to get down to the substance of our deepest desire to see whether it is truly healthy and is taking us in the direction of peace and freedom. Otherwise, we are going in the direction of suffering and despair. We should know whether we are being a true or a false bodhisattva. We have to be certain that our actions bring real well-being, peace, and compassion.

Consciousness: The Fourth Food

The fourth kind of food is consciousness. If we allow ourselves to be nourished by delusion, ignorance, fear, and violence, our consciousness will bring about the kind of life that makes us and those around us suffer. By ingesting the right kinds of mental, physical, and spiritual food, we grow in wisdom, compassion, and nonviolence. We become mindful of our consumer behavior so that we support the well-being of our society and civilization.

For the fourth kind of food, consciousness, the Buddha gave us the example of a gentleman who was sentenced to death for his criminal deeds. On the morning of his execution, the king ordered the soldiers to pierce the man with one hundred swords. At noon the soldiers reported that the man was still alive, and the king ordered them to pierce him again with one hundred swords. In the evening, the soldiers reported that the man was still alive, and the king ordered his soldiers to pierce him again with one hundred swords, and again the man survived. When we consume unmindfully, it is as if we are stabbing ourselves morning, noon, and night with one hundred swords, damaging not only ourselves but all our ancestors and all our descendants.

Looking back on history, we see that many civilizations have destroyed themselves. Our civilization will be no different if we do not wake up. We have to wake up so we can stop the course of destruction brought on by our unmindful way of living. To learn the way out, we have to look carefully as members of communities, cities, and nations, and as members of our planet into what and how we are consuming. And we have to do this collectively. Our survival is no longer an individual matter.

CHAPTER FOUR

RIGHT ACTION COMES FROM RIGHT UNDERSTANDING

In 1968 I was in the United States to call for cessation of the American bombing in Vietnam. In May of that year, the bombing of Saigon became so fierce that the whole area around the School of Youth for Social Service, which my students and I had organized, was destroyed. More than ten thousand refugees came to the campus, many of them wounded, and we had to take care of them. We were not at all equipped for this in terms of food, basic hygiene, and medical supplies, and it was very dangerous to travel outside the campus to get provisions. When we had used up our supply of bandages, the young women tore their long dresses to make more bandages.

In this desperate situation, we had to evacuate the seriously wounded from our campus. But to do so, we had to cross the battle zone to bring them to the hospital. We decided to use the five-colored Buddhist flag to replace the Red Cross flag. The monks and nuns put on their sanghatis, their monastic ceremonial robes, and carried out the wounded. The Buddhist flag and the sanghati robes signaled that we were a peaceful group. Fortunately, it worked and we were able to evacuate these patients; otherwise, many would have died.

On the third day of the bombing, panic broke out on our overcrowded campus: there was a rumor that the anti-Communists were going to bomb the school because there were so many Communists among the refugees. When people heard this, many collected their belongings and started to leave, but the bombing was so heavy they were driven back. The Communists and the anti-Communists were fighting at the very edge of our campus. At that moment Thay Thanh Van, a twenty-five-year-old monk and the school's director, took a large megaphone and was about to announce that people should not leave when he suddenly asked himself, "What if the bombing really takes place?" Thousands of people would die, and how could the young monk bear such a responsibility? So he slowly put down the megaphone and did not make the announcement.

Thay Thanh Van realized that he needed to speak to both warring parties. To do this, he had to crawl across the fire zone; otherwise, one side or the other would have shot him. First he went to the anti-Communists and persuaded the commanding officer to instruct their planes not to bomb the campus filled with refugees. Then he went to the Communist guerrillas, who had set up antiaircraft guns just at the corner of the campus. He asked them not to shoot at enemy planes; otherwise the campus would be bombed in retaliation. Both sides were moved by his request and did as he asked. It was a miracle. On this mission he did not carry anything with him except his courage, love, and compassion.

In a situation like that, you have to be extremely mindful. Sometimes you have to react quickly while remaining calm, but if you were angry or suspicious, you could not do this. You have to be clear-minded. In the context of war, we grew deeper in our practice of nonviolence. Nonviolence is not a set of techniques that you can learn with your intellect. Nonviolent action is born naturally from compassion, lucidity, and understanding within yourself.

The Basis of Right Action:
The Four Noble Truths

The Buddha always taught that we should practice the Four Noble Truths:

1. There is suffering.
2. There is an origin of suffering.
3. The end of suffering is possible.
4. There is a path to the end of suffering.

With the practice of mindfulness we are already working with the Four Noble Truths. When we practice mindfulness, we learn to stop and to calm ourselves; then we naturally recognize our suffering and the suffering of others. By looking deeply we see into the causes of suffering and the way to transform our suffering and the suffering of others. When you can transform the war and violence in yourself, then you can truly begin to help others find peace.

Suffering is a part of life. As bodhisattvas in training, we have vowed to use our Mind of Love to alleviate and transform suffering. By listening deeply to those who suffer, by recognizing suffering and the roots of suffering, we put into action the First and Second Noble Truths. By looking deeply, we can see the cause of suffering, we can see that it's possible to end suffering, and we can also see the path that leads to the end of suffering. This puts into action the Third and Fourth Noble Truths.

Taking action to stop suffering is Right Action. Understanding is the foundation of every good action. No action can be called Right Action without Right Understanding. In order to understand, we have to listen, but how do we know we have Right Understanding? If you try to help someone but your actions only worsen the situation, then you did not have Right Understanding. If your government passes an unjust law, it is because your representatives did not have Right Understanding of the problem they were trying to address. All actions—all our personal, political, and humanitarian activities—must be based on a clear understanding of yourself, of your situation, of your own people, of your country.

Deep listening and loving speech are wonderful instruments to help us arrive at the kind of understanding we all need as a basis for appropriate action. You listen deeply for only one purpose—to allow the other person to empty his or her heart. This is already an act of relieving suffering. To stop any suffering, no matter how small, is a great action of peace. The path to end suffering depends on your understanding and your capacity to act without causing harm or further suffering. This is acting with compassion, your best protection.

IN 1964 I WAS on my way to Da Nang to survey relief work for flood victims. I had to take a military plane because there were no flights for civilians. While I was waiting on the military airfield, an American army officer arrived to wait for his plane. It was just the two of us on the airfield. I wanted to speak to him because I could see he was lonely and worried. Out of compassion, I asked him if he were afraid of the Vietcong, the Communist guerrillas. Immediately I realized that I had made a big mistake: my question touched off his fear. To American soldiers, guerrillas were everywhere. They all felt they could be ambushed and killed at any time. My question made him shiver. He put his hand on his gun and asked, "Are you a Vietcong?"

Because I listened deeply to him, I was aware of what was going on in him. I kept still and just followed my breathing. With a calm and quiet voice, I explained that I was a monk from Saigon on my way to help flood victims. By speaking in such a mindful way, I was able to restore his calm. Had I not taken this care, he might have shot me right there, simply out of fear. But we were able to overcome his fear, and we continued our journey with a little more understanding between us.

Misperception Is the Enemy

Our enemy is never another person; our enemy is the wrong perceptions and suffering within him, within her. When a doctor sees a person who is suffering, he tries to identify the sickness within the patient, to remove it. He does not try to kill his patient. The role of the doctor is not to kill people but to cure the illnesses within them. It is the same with a person who has suffered so much and who has been making you suffer—the solution is not to kill him but to try to relieve him of his suffering. This is the guidance of our spiritual teachers. It is the practice of understanding and love. In order to love truly, we must first understand.

When You Have Difficulty with Someone, Both of You Suffer

When you suffer, you must practice to find the cause of the suffering within yourself and the other person. You must reflect on your emotions, transform them, and then be willing to listen to the other person. Then you must take Right Action to eliminate the causes. If you can help the other person remove the roots of suffering within herself, then she will no longer suffer, and she will stop making you suffer.

Perhaps a friend has been making you suffer by what she has said and done. Her speech is full of bitterness, wrong perceptions, condemnation, and blame, and because of this you suffer very much. You also suffer because of her way of thinking. You have to remember, however, that you are not the only one who is suffering. Keep in mind that this person may have suffered very deeply in order to speak that way, to do things like that. If this person were not suffering, she would not say and do such things. This is a simple insight, but perhaps you do not see it because of your own pain. If you understand this, then you will try your best to help her not to suffer. When she no longer suffers, she will leave you in peace; you will no longer suffer. Helping her is helping yourself. This is very clear and very simple. You have to recognize that the other person is suffering, that you are not the only one. Looking deeply, you recognize that if the other person continues to suffer, you will continue to suffer as well.

You may try going to the other person and saying, "My dear friend, I know that you have suffered quite a lot in the past. I'm sorry I did not understand your suffering, and I have contributed to it by my way of reacting to what you have said and done. I don't want you to suffer. I don't want to destroy you. I really want you to be happy, because I know that if you are happy, I'll have a chance to be happy, too. I know that you have a lot of perceptions and ideas about me. You must have thought of me as evil, as a monster. I am sorry. Because I didn't understand your suffering, I wasn't able to help you, and I have made the situation worse. I'm very sorry; I don't want this to continue.

"If you care to talk to me, if you care to tell me what is in your heart, what were the unskillful things that I have done to you, then I promise that I will do my best to help you and in the future refrain from doing and saying the things that make you and me suffer." This is the practice, and if you are honest and you say it with all your heart and you are motivated by the desire to help, then the other person will open up and tell you what is in her heart.

Escalation of Peace

Suffering, unhappiness, violence, and war escalate when we are overcome with anger and try to punish and inflict suffering on the other side. We act this way because we believe that as a result we will suffer less, but of course this action only leads to the other side desiring revenge. This is the surest course of destruction. Deep down, we know this is childish, unintelligent behavior, but still most of us act this way. When we suffer, we blame the other person or group. We hope that if we can punish them and make them suffer, we will feel better and gain some relief. We know the disastrous effects of such behavior, yet we continue to follow this course. The result is more unhappiness, more terrorism, more violence, and more war.

Sometimes, people who cannot find any way to resolve a problem with someone else are tempted to eliminate the problem by eliminating the other person. They wish the other person would just go away, die, or disappear. That desire may be strong enough to lead them to kill. Killing another person is not an act of freedom but an act of despair and great ignorance; it will not bring freedom or peace.

Let us train ourselves to act with Right Understanding and compassion and move in the opposite direction. We can live our lives in such a way that we cause an escalation of peace to occur within our family, our school, and our society. Offering a calm and gentle smile—this is an act of peace. Looking with the eyes of compassion, making a peaceful step—these are gestures of peace and nonviolence that you can offer every day. Speak peacefully, walk peacefully, think peacefully, and your peace will radiate out in all directions.

Deep Listening

Deep, compassionate listening is essential to the creation of peace—personal, interpersonal, community, national, and international peace. In this practice you listen with all your mindfulness and concentration in order to give someone who is suffering a chance to speak out. Even if his speech is full of condemnation, bitterness, and blame, you still listen, because you know that to listen like this is to give him a chance to move in the direction of peace. If you interrupt, deny, or correct everything he says, he will have no chance to make peace. Deep listening allows the other person to speak, even if what he says contains wrong perceptions, bitterness, and injustice.

The intention of listening is to restore communication, because once communication is restored, everything is possible. I have seen many couples practice deep listening and loving speech and restore difficult or broken relationships. Many fathers and sons, mothers and daughters, and husbands and wives have brought happiness back to their families through this practice. They have practiced mindful breathing and walking to calm themselves. Then, with the practice of deep, compassionate listening and loving speech, they have reconciled.

Listening to someone with compassion can turn her into a friend. It may be that no one else has been able to listen to her; perhaps you are the first one capable of listening to her and giving her the relief she needs. You become a bodhisattva, a being who ends suffering. You lose an enemy and win a friend.

During the war in Vietnam, both sides operated and reacted out of fear. During any war—the war within you, the war with your parents, partner, children, the war with your neighbors, a war between nations—we act and react out of fear. When you act out of fear, you cause harm and destruction to yourself and others. Fear is a product of ignorance and lack of compassion, which are the very atmosphere of war. Fear feeds off ignorance, whereas compassion and lucidity flower from understanding. Deep listening and loving speech can stop new anger and fear from arising as well as transform long-held misperceptions and suffering. With mindfulness, we can protect ourselves from danger.

Lotus in a Sea of Fire: Engaged Buddhism

From a very young age, I had a strong desire to put the Buddha's teachings into practice in order to improve the lives of the people around me, especially those of the poor peasants. Many monks, including myself, had a deep desire to bring Buddhism into every walk of life. For us, taking action according to the principles of what I called Engaged Buddhism—Right action based in compassion—was the answer.

I started reflecting and writing on the possibility and practice of Engaged Buddhism in the 1950s, and in 1964 I wrote the book *Engaged Buddhism.* In an essay titled "The Basic Ideals of Buddhist Youth for Social Service," I suggested how to apply Buddhist ideals to improve the conditions of life in a time of war and social injustice. In a later book, *Actualized Buddhism,* I advocated a kind of Buddhism that could be practiced in all areas of life: economics, education, and art, among others. These writings document the birth of the Engaged Buddhism movement in Vietnam. Engaged Buddhism was a product of suffering and war—a lotus flower blooming in a sea of fire.

As a novice, I understood that social work could not be successful if the people engaged in it were not calm and solid in their practice of mindfulness and compassion. I knew even then that social workers and social activists had to transform their own suffering and cultivate freedom of mind and spirit and lead a simple life to be effective. I also knew personally how challenging that was, particularly in a time of war.

In those years practitioners in the monasteries particularly felt the suffering of the people around us. When the warplanes came and dropped bombs around us, we heard the sounds of our people crying out in pain and anguish. There were wounded children and destroyed houses and refugees to take care of. We could not ignore them and just sit quietly in our meditation halls. We had to go out and help, but we knew we would become exhausted if we did these things without nurturing our own spirit. We set aside one day a week as a Day of Mindfulness so we could nourish and sustain ourselves as we brought relief to the people suffering around us. We used the teachings of the Buddha about self-protection and self-healing in our personal practice and then took them out into the world. This was Engaged Buddhism in its purest form.

Self-Help Villages

As part of our practice of Engaged Buddhism during the war in Vietnam, we set up self-help villages on the front lines. We studied the kibbutzim in Israel to learn from their experience of communal living, which combined family life with the life of the village. We learned which activities would best unfold in the context of the family unit, and in which ones all the people in the village would participate. We tried to combine collective and individual efforts to increase harmony and to share expenses.

For instance, each villager had his own plot of land to grow vegetables; in addition, there were lands that belonged to the entire community. Sometimes villagers worked on their own plots of land, and sometimes they worked together with other families on communal land. In this way it was not necessary for every family to buy every piece of farm equipment. The whole community owned and shared a tractor, and every family had the right to borrow it for their own use. There were also community-owned cars that could be used by anyone on occasion. This sharing not only saved money but also helped the people in the village to establish deeper relationships with other families in the community.

We could offer only a small amount of financial aid to these villages, as we ourselves did not have much, yet we were still able to be of help with our goodwill, technical knowledge, concern, and loving-kindness. Because of the ongoing war, we knew it would be a long time before we could receive help from the government.

In the early 1960s I visited India, the Philippines, and other countries to make inquiries about other ways to help community development, and in 1964 a group of friends and I set up the School of Youth for Social Service in Vietnam. Our program was focused on four areas: rural education, health, economics, and organization. Our guiding principle was to begin with what we had and what we knew. Combining the technical know-how of our social workers with that of the farmers, we were immediately able to improve the quality of the villagers' lives.

When we announced the opening of the School of Youth for Social Service, hundreds of young people volunteered. They were eager to help and wanted to be trained right away. Among them were monks and nuns and students about to graduate from medical, law, and other professional schools. The students' expertise proved very useful. For example, many of the village children did not have birth certificates, which at that time were required to enroll in public school. Though we had set up our own schools in the villages, we wanted some of the children to be able to go to public school. To issue a birth certificate, a judge and two witnesses were needed. One day the law students brought a judge into one of our pilot villages, and we arranged an open-air meeting place where the judge and witnesses could work. We quickly issued dozens of birth certificates.

We also set up simple health centers under thatched roofs, each with only one doctor and a few nurses. For the first time, people in the villages did not have to wait for months for needed medical treatment. This was a revolutionary solution at that time and place. There was an atmosphere of great joy among us because we were able to do so much for the people.

One night as I slept in the small thatched house of a peasant, a scorpion came out from under the roof and bit me. It was very painful. I did not have any ointment or medicine with me, so I had to massage the wound for hours to survive the night. This was the condition that peasants lived in all the time. Many of the children had diseases and often had trouble with their eyes. Every Saturday and Sunday, we invited a doctor and a nurse to come to a village to treat these children with the assistance of the recently graduated medical students. These kinds of experiences gave those of us who practiced Engaged Buddhism realistic insights into how to help.

As social workers from the School of Youth for Social Service, we came into the villages dressed more or less like peasants. It was important not to dress like city people, because government officials came to the villages dressed as city people, creating an immediate gap between them and the poor peasants.

As social workers we began with the children. We talked to them and won their sympathy. We would teach them how to sing, how to read the alphabet and to write. We did not need a schoolhouse. We just sat down under a tree and played with the children. We cut their nails and bathed them in the river. When parents saw that we were helping their children read and write, they became grateful, and we won their hearts as well. Then, when it rained and we had to move our classes indoors, a villager would allow us to run into his or her house for cover.

Soon we had a big group of children who wanted to learn, and we asked the villagers to help set up a school. One family would agree to give a piece of land, another promised to give twenty bamboo trees, and still another family gave fifty coconut leaves to make the roof. In a short time we had the collaboration of everyone in the village. Setting up a school like this was rewarding and joyful. We would have had to wait a long time for the government, so we did it on our own, beginning with what we had and what we knew. The peasants knew how to build their own houses, so they were perfectly capable of building a beautiful school.

In Binh Khanh village in the province of Gia Dinh, I participated in building the people's first school ever, which we called the Nightingale School. I taught the students and the young monks and nuns how to construct the building to keep the heat inside. We made the walls with bamboo and finished by putting mud and straw around them. Inside it was warm and cozy during cold weather. When villagers establish and build a school with their own hands, they protect it, and if repairs are needed they do the maintenance themselves. No one can come and destroy or close down the school. If it had been a government school, however, the villagers would not have protected it with the kind of love they had for what they themselves had created.

The School of Youth for Social Service workers took turns leading class. Later we hired a teacher, offering a small salary, just enough for him or her to live simply. Yet the teacher was content, because instructing children and making them happy was reward enough.

Not only did we teach children but we also helped the adults. We offered night courses so they could learn to read, write, and study subjects crucial to their health and living. We brought technicians into the village to teach better ways to take care of chickens and pigs, how to make compost, and how to organize a cooperative.

We shared a great deal of knowledge with the farmers so they could organize themselves in the areas of education, health, and economics. We suggested making various handicrafts that could bring additional income to the families. We also helped the villagers organize entertainment, like music and concerts for the children and young adults. Otherwise, they might have grown bored with village life and moved to the city, leaving the countryside bereft of young people. We set up libraries and organized festivals like the full moon festival. We also offered vocational training for the young people to learn traditional skills.

In six months we were able to transform a village. The young people and the Buddhist monks and nuns liked this kind of social work very much. To this day, we continue to support this kind of work for village development in Vietnam in spite of difficulties under the current regime.

Compassion and loving-kindness are not philosophical notions; they are translated into daily reality. These efforts are compassion in action.

Even the Buddha Goes Out to Help

There was a young man named An in our School of Youth for Social Service. When he came to the villages, he taught the children to read, and he also cared for the sick late into the night. He worked so diligently that a woman asked him how much he earned for his work from the government. He replied, "I'm not an employee of the government. I am a Buddhist. We are working to perform merits." "Performing merits" is a popular term in Buddhism, used by laypeople who offer their time and energy to help with temple work. The woman said, "People get merit in the temple, not out here." The young man replied, "Dear Aunt, in this time of suffering, we choose to perform merits here and not in the temple. The children have no one who cares for them. I believe that serving them is serving the Buddha." The woman understood right away what An was saying and wholeheartedly supported our efforts. An's statement is a wonderful and simple explanation of Engaged Buddhism.

In the School of Youth for Social Service, I did not teach traditional Buddhism. Instead I taught students how a social worker should behave when he is sent to a village, how she can win the hearts of children and adults. I taught that they first had to win the trust of a family, behaving like sons or daughters of the family so that they could become fully integrated. Once a family accepted them, they were protected. The family they stayed with should be trusted and respected by the villagers. Once they were aligned with a family who loved, trusted, and protected them, they could begin to contribute to the life of the village.

We tried not to offer money to villagers. Instead the workers had to go to the villages empty-handed. The first thing they offered was their deep listening. After coming to understand the needs of the villagers, the workers offered their knowledge and love. Our policy was to help people to learn to help themselves. We offered money only after the villagers were already empowered to take care of their situations.

Once our social workers had been accepted by a family, they had to win the support of the Buddhist temple in the area. Most Vietnamese people are Buddhist, so in each village there is a temple, the spiritual home of the village. With the support of the temple, the social workers would not have difficulties. They spent time with the senior monk and told him where they had come from and what their intentions were. If the monk accepted them, they could succeed in helping the village.

Practicing Engaged Buddhism Today

If you want to become a social worker, you can adapt these principles to your own community and country. If you live in a country where Christianity is the main religion and wish to perform community service, you can go to the Protestant minister or the Catholic priest in your area. You can help the community and then ask the temple or church to shelter you and your fellow workers, to allow you to sponsor classes for adults or children.

Your knowledge and experience of the practice of mindfulness is crucial; it lies at the heart of your ability to taken Right Action and engage with the world. You have to train yourself to be an agent of peace and reconciliation wherever you are—in your host family or church or temple. You are teaching the way of mindfulness without the title of teacher. You are doing social work without the title of social worker. You are nobody at all, but you can be everything to the people who need your help.

There is a mathematics teacher from North America who has come to several retreats at Plum Village. He was always an excellent teacher, but for many years he had a difficult time in his classroom because he would become angry easily. Before he learned the practice of nonviolence, he used to yell or throw chalk at his students when they upset him. Sometimes in fits of irritation he would write comments on their homework such as "How can you be so stupid?"

After he had practiced mindfulness for a while, he transformed dramatically. He entered the classroom in slow walking meditation. He went over to the blackboard and erased everything in a mindful way. His surprised students asked, "Teacher, are you sick?" He replied with a smile: "No, I'm not sick, I'm just trying to do things mindfully." He shared the practice of mindfulness with them, proposing that every fifteen minutes a student should clap his hands so that the entire class could stop and practice breathing and smiling. His students enjoyed practicing with him and grew to love him more and more. Instead of writing on their work, "How can you be so stupid?" he now wrote, "You don't understand, it's my fault." His class made great progress. Soon every class in the school adopted his techniques. When he reached retirement age, this teacher was asked to stay on for a few more years. He is now a mindfulness teacher—and a mindful teacher.

This is a real example of practice, of progress, and of peace. Slowly, with mindful action, we can transform ourselves, our family, school, workplace, neighborhood, city hall, national government, and the global community. If you are a schoolteacher, a parent, a journalist, a therapist, or a writer, you can use your talent to promote this change. We should practice meditation collectively, because looking deeply into our situation is no longer an individual matter. We have to combine our individual insights into collective wisdom.

A Nonviolent Army

During the war in Vietnam, we in the School of Youth for Social Service often worked in dangerous places. Because we won the hearts of the people so easily, each warring party suspected us of belonging to the other side and wanted to eliminate us. Both sides were afraid of us. They thought we had a political motive, but we did not. In a situation of war, practitioners of peace do not take sides. Instead, they promote reconciliation and try to bring the two sides together. This is a very dangerous position to take. Even though we were motivated only by our Bodhicitta, the Mind of Love, both warring parties did not understand and killed many of us.

Yet it was misunderstanding that was the killer. We were a nonviolent army that carried only love and our intention to help as our weapons, but we suffered casualties just like other armies. Brother Nhat Tri, along with seven other social workers, was murdered while traveling to a remote village. I considered them all my sons and daughters and felt just as a father would who had lost eight children of his own blood at once. I suffered tremendously, and the marks of this suffering are in many of my poems.

I wrote this poem in 1965 especially for the young people in the School of Youth for Social Service who risked their lives every day during the war, recommending that they prepare to die without hatred. Some had already been killed violently, and I cautioned the others against hating. Our enemy is our anger, hatred, greed, fanaticism, and discrimination, I told them. If you die because of violence, you must meditate on compassion in order to forgive those who killed you. When you die realizing this state of compassion, you are truly a child of the Awakened One. Even if you are dying in oppression, shame, and violence, if you can smile with forgiveness, you have great power.

Rereading the lines of this poem, I suddenly understood the passage in the "Diamond Sutra" that speaks about *ksanti,* endurance or tolerance:

> *Your courage intact, your eyes kind,*
> *Untroubled*
> *(Even as no one sees them),*
> *Out of your smile*
> *Will bloom a flower.*

And those who love you
Will behold you
Across ten thousand worlds of birth and dying.

If you die with compassion in mind, you are a torch lighting our path.

RECOMMENDATION

Promise me,
promise me this day,
promise me now,
while the sun is overhead
exactly at the zenith,
promise me:

Even as they
strike you down
with a mountain of hatred and violence;
even as they step on you and crush you
like a worm,
even as they dismember and disembowel you,
remember, brother,
remember:
man is not our enemy.

The only thing worthy of you is compassion—
invincible, limitless, unconditional.
Hatred will never let you face
the beast in man.

One day, when you face this beast alone,
with your courage intact, your eyes kind,
untroubled
(even as no one sees them),
out of your smile
will bloom a flower.
And those who love you
will behold you
across ten thousand worlds of birth and dying.

Alone again,
I will go on with bent head,
knowing that love has become eternal.
On the long, rough road,
the sun and the moon
will continue to shine.

Tragedy from misunderstanding happened much more than that once. The first time our workers were massacred by one of the warring parties was when some soldiers came to the School of Youth for Social Service campus heavily armed and threw grenades into our dormitories, killing two social workers, both young women. Another young woman was extensively wounded— three hundred pieces of shrapnel entered her body. That night she lost most of her blood and almost died. The hospital was four hours away and, in any event, had no blood bank. Masako Yamanouchi, a Japanese volunteer who worked with us, saved the wounded student's life by donating blood. The wounded woman had to be treated in both Vietnam and Japan for several years, and she still carries within her more than one hundred pieces of shrapnel.

One night in 1966, a group of armed men came to a village where six of our young men were staying. They went to the house, woke them up, tied their hands, and brought them to the river-bank. Although they took our workers by force, they did not speak harshly to them. At the riverbank, the armed men asked our workers whether they were part of the School of Youth for Social Service. They answered yes. The men asked a second time to make sure and then said to our friends, "We are very sorry, we have to kill you." They then shot all six of them on the riverbank. They had received orders from their superiors, who considered us their enemies, to kill anyone from our school because we had dared to work in the villages.

The armed men thought they had killed the whole group, but one of them survived. The next day Sister Chan Khong, my student and later one of the cofounders of Plum Village, went with a number of our other friends and carried the surviving young man to the hospital, where he told them what had happened.

Although we had come with pure hearts, they mistook us as their enemies. We just wanted to love and to help. We did not have any political motive, yet we were victims of suspicion and vi-olence.

When the attack happened, I was in Paris. I was preparing to give a series of talks in France, the United States, Australia, New Zealand, the Philippines, and Japan. The night I heard that five of my students had been murdered, I could not even cry. It took many months before I was able to do so. These young people, too, were my children. They had listened to my teachings on Engaged Buddhism and joined with us to serve, and then suddenly they died. It was a difficult time for me and for all of the members of our group. I needed to practice and transform my suffering before I could voice my grief. It was only months later, in New York City, after I had finished writing the play *The Path of Return Continues the Journey,* that I could begin to cry—and as I cried, I began to release my pain.

After each attack Sister Chan Khong and other leaders of the School organized funerals where they read a text confirming that our intention was only to love and help, not to hate or kill. They would read, "Dear friends, you don't understand us, and that is why you have killed us. Our intention is not to do harm to anyone. We only want to help." There was neither bitterness nor hate in our speech.

Sometimes when villages were bombed, our social workers feared for their lives and wanted to flee. But I had asked them not to abandon the peasants because, unlike them, the villagers could not escape the situation. So the social workers stayed and helped rebuild the bombed villages. When the same villages were bombed again, we patiently rebuilt them once more. It was important to restore the houses, but it was even more important to give our psychological support to the villagers so that they would not give up hope.

During this time of great loss, I was again back in Paris, but I knew our friends and colleagues in the School of Youth for Social Services were undergoing difficult times in Vietnam. Nevertheless, I trusted that they would overcome. We actually were able to suffer less than the people who considered us their enemies because we held fast to the spirit of openness, love, and compassion. Our diligent, solid practice of love and mindfulness after each attack eventually moved the hearts of the killers and they stopped trying to kill us. Ultimately, our loving speech showed them that we were not their enemy.

Compassion Is the Best Protection

To understand both sides in a conflict, and to see what to do and what not to do, we must have confidence in our own view, in our own experiences and understanding of the difference between truth and wrong perceptions. We must be able to withstand the influence of public opinion and propaganda. This strength comes from looking deeply with compassion and from solid practice. Those who make the news and those who make political strategies have a strong effect on us. Political parties and politicians are always trying to persuade us. They try to change the way we think and feel, so we must be rooted in ourselves and our practice, looking deeply so that we will not be misled. If we do not maintain our own stability and insight, we can be easily swayed. Please remember that Right Action comes only from Right Understanding and that we must practice deep listening in order to understand. With this in mind you become a bodhisattva of peace and reconciliation.

RECONCILIATION

PEACE PRACTICES FOR INDIVIDUALS
AND PARTNERS

King Bimbisara, the ruler of a kingdom in what is now India, was one of the Buddha's closest friends and students. One day the Buddha was informed by a monk that King Bimbisara had abdicated the throne in favor of his son, Prince Ajatasattu, and was under house arrest.

Queen Videhi, the king's wife, came to see the Buddha and told him that, a month earlier, the imperial guards had caught the prince about to enter the king's chambers late one night. Finding his behavior suspicious, they searched him and discovered a sword concealed under his robes. They seized him and took him into the king's room. The king looked at his son and asked, "Ajatasattu, why were you carrying a sword into my chamber?"

"It was my intention to kill you," answered Ajatasattu.

"But why would you want to kill me?"

"I want to be king."

"Why must you kill your own father to be king? If you had but asked me, I would have abdicated at once."

"I did not think you would do that. I made a grave error, and I beg you to forgive me."

Although it was the middle of the night, the king then summoned his two most trusted counselors. One adviser said that trying to assassinate the king was a crime punishable by death and the prince should be beheaded.

The king disagreed. "I cannot kill Ajatasattu. He is my own son."

The second adviser said, "Your compassion has no equal, Your Majesty! You are a worthy student of the Lord Buddha's. But how do you propose to deal with this matter?"

The king said, "Tomorrow I will let it be known to the people that I am abdicating the throne in favor of my son. His coronation can take place in ten days."

"But what of his crime of attempted assassination?"

"I forgive him. I hope he will learn something from this."

Two days after the king's decision to abdicate, Ajatasattu placed his father under house arrest. The queen said to the Buddha, "The king's life is in grave danger. Ajatasattu plans to starve him to death. He will not allow me to bring any food to my husband." She told the Buddha that, even though she had wept when she saw the king, Bimbisara had consoled her and told her that he bore no hatred toward their son for his actions. He said he would rather suffer hunger than have the country plunged into civil war.

The Buddha sat silently as the queen began to sob. After a

long moment, he asked about the king's state of health, both physical and spiritual. The queen said that although he had lost a lot of weight, his strength was holding up, and his spirit was high. He expressed no feelings of hatred or regret. He continued to smile and carry on a conversation as if nothing had happened. He was using his time as a prisoner to practice meditation. There was a long corridor in his chamber where he did walking meditation. The room also had a window that faced Vulture Peak, and every day for long periods he gazed at the mountain as he did sitting meditation.

Several weeks later the Buddha learned that the king had died of starvation.

Some months after his father's death, King Ajatasattu's army invaded one of the territories of King Pasendadi, his mother's brother. The war raged on for six months, with many casualties on both sides, but ultimately King Pasendadi's armies were victorious and King Ajatasattu was captured alive.

Afterward King Pasendadi visited the Buddha. He described the terrible cost of the war. "Lord Buddha, King Ajatasattu killed his own father to usurp the throne and invaded my country. But he is my own nephew. I cannot kill him, nor do I have any desire to put him in prison. Please help me find a wise course of action."

The Buddha said, "Your Majesty, you are surrounded by loyal friends and aides. It is no surprise that you came out the victor in this war. King Ajatasattu is surrounded by bad elements, and so he has gone astray. I suggest you treat him with all the respect due a king. Take time, as well, to guide him as your nephew. Strongly impress on him the importance of surrounding himself with friends and aides of good and loyal character. Then you can send him back to his kingdom. The possibility of lasting peace depends on your skill in handling these matters."

Shortly afterward King Ajatasattu was released and allowed to return to rule his kingdom. Using love to ease the wounds of hatred, King Pasendadi gave his own daughter, Princess Varaja, in marriage to Ajatasattu, making him his son-in-law as well as his nephew. Wholeheartedly following the spirit of the Buddha's counsel, King Pasendadi also gave back to Ajatasattu the land he had won in the war as a wedding gift.

After returning to his kingdom, King Ajatasattu suffered from extreme mental anguish. He was haunted by his father's death, and his mind could find no ease. His nerves were constantly on edge, and he was afraid to sleep at night because of the terrible nightmares that came to him. Many doctors and high-ranking priests were summoned to cure him, but for three years Ajatasattu's mental anguish worsened daily. One day the king ate dinner with his wife; their son, Udayibhadda; and his mother, Queen Videhi. Prince Udayibhadda was almost three years old, and because the king catered to his every whim, he was an unruly, spoiled child. The prince demanded that his dog be allowed to sit at the dinner table, and although such a thing was normally forbidden, the king gave in to his son's wish. Feeling somewhat embarrassed, the king said to his own mother, "It is unpleasant having a dog sitting at the table, isn't it, but what else can I do?"

Queen Videhi answered, "You love your son, and so you have allowed him to bring his dog to the table. There is nothing unusual about that. Do you remember how your own father once healed your hand because he loved you?"

Ajatasattu did not recall the incident. The queen told him, "One day when you were a little boy, your finger became red and swollen. A boil formed underneath your fingernail. It caused you so much pain, you cried all day and night. Your father was unable to sleep out of concern for you. He lifted you onto his pillow and placed your infected finger in his mouth. He sucked on it to help relieve the pain. He sucked on your finger throughout four days and nights until the boil broke, and then he sucked out the pus. He did not dare remove your finger from his mouth to spit out the pus for fear you would feel more pain. And so he swallowed the pus while continuing to suck on your finger. You see how deeply your father loved you."

The king suddenly clutched his head in his two hands and ran from the room. Afterward, his mental state worsened. The physician Jivaka was summoned. Jivaka listened to Ajatasattu recount all his woes and how no priest or doctor had been able to help him, and he sat without saying a word. The king asked, "Jivaka, why don't you say anything?"

Jivaka replied, "The Buddha is the only person who can help you overcome the agony in your heart. Go to the Buddha for guidance."

The king did not speak for several minutes. Finally he muttered, "But I am sure he hates me."

Jivaka replied, "The Buddha does not hate anyone. He was your father's teacher and closest friend. Going to him will be like going to your own father. See him and you will find peace. My ability to heal is nothing compared with the Buddha's."

The king agreed, and it was arranged that Ajatasattu would meet the Buddha at his meditation hall. On a moonlit night, the king, seated on an elephant, proceeded to the meeting with a great entourage. When he approached the meditation hall, everything was still. Jivaka had told him that there were a thousand monks living with the Buddha. If this were true, thought Ajatasattu, how could it be so quiet? Could it be a trick? Was he being led into an ambush? He turned to Jivaka and asked if this was a plot to seek revenge for the killing of his father.

Jivaka laughed and pointed to the meditation hall, from whose windows light was streaming. Jivaka said, "The Buddha and all his monks are in there this very moment."

The king climbed down from his elephant and entered the hall, followed by his family and attendants. Jivaka pointed to a man sitting on a platform, his back supported against a pillar, and said, "There is the Buddha."

The king was impressed by the attentive quiet. A thousand monks surrounded the Buddha in perfect silence. Not even a robe rustled.

The Buddha invited the king to be seated. The king bowed and then spoke. "Lord, I remember hearing you speak at the palace when I was a boy. Tonight, I would like to ask you a question. What kinds of fruit does the spiritual life bear that hundreds, even thousands, abandon their homes to pursue it?"

The Buddha asked the king if he had ever asked any other teachers the same question. The king responded that he had, in fact, asked dozens, but he had never received a satisfactory answer.

The Buddha said, "Your Majesty, I will tell you the fruits that can be found in this teaching, fruits that can be enjoyed in this very moment, and fruits that can be reaped in the future. You need not seek lofty answers. Simply look and see these fruits as clearly as a mango held in your hand.

"Consider this; a monk observes a series of practices that enable him to dwell in calm and peace. People who do not observe such practices are easily misguided. They commit crimes such as lying, drunkenness, sexual misconduct, stealing, and even murder. They bring cruel punishment on their minds and bodies. These practices help prevent us from falling into error, thus assuring a carefree state.

"Your Majesty, a monk owns few possessions, and so he has no fear of losing his possessions or being robbed. He is free to sleep alone in the forest beneath a tree, relaxed and without worries. Freedom from fear is great happiness. A monk does not chase after wealth or fame. He uses only what he needs and remains unattached to desires. Living in such carefree ease is great happiness. That is another fruit of spiritual practice which can be enjoyed right here in the present moment.

"If you knew how to practice full awareness of breathing and how to meditate, you could experience the happiness of one who follows the path. It is the happiness that meditation brings. Through meditation we can use full awareness of breathing to create joy and happiness that nourishes our mind and body and helps us to make progress on the path of enlightenment. The joy and happiness of meditation permeates mind and body, heals all anxiety, sorrow, and despair, and enables the practitioner to experience the wonders of life. With meditation you cut through the ropes of bondage which bind most people—the ropes of greed, hatred, desire, laziness, doubt, false view of self, extreme views, wrong views, and distorted views. Liberation is a great happiness and one of the greatest fruits of spiritual practice. This fruit can be attained right here in this life.

"Thanks to this understanding, the practitioner does not need to worry or fear. Through his inner peace he is able to help others free themselves from the maze of desire, hatred, and ignorance. A monk does not engage in partisan politics but contributes to building peace, joy, and virtue in society. The fruits of his spiritual practice are not for any individual's sole enjoyment and benefit. They are humanity's and the world's inheritance."

The king stood up and joined his palms in deepest respect. He said, "Most sublime teacher! With your simple words, you have rebuilt what was in ruins, revealed what was concealed, shown the way to one who was lost, and brought light into the darkness. Please accept me as your disciple, as you accepted my parents in the past."

The Buddha nodded his acceptance.

After this, the king visited the Buddha often. In these meetings the Buddha treated Ajatasattu as though he were his own son, which allowed the king to reveal his heart and confess his past crimes. The night after their first meeting, Ajatasattu dreamed he saw his father smiling at him and felt all had been made whole again. The king's heart was transformed.

Beginning Anew: The Practice of Reconciliation and Renewal

As human beings, we all make mistakes. Our unskillful thoughts, words, and actions cause harm to ourselves and those around us.

Often, when we hurt others or are hurt by them, because of our pride we make no effort to reconcile or renew our relationships. Without reconciliation, we cannot deepen our understanding and we only cause more suffering.

Our practice is to renew our relationships on a regular basis. Every week we have time to go to concerts, cinema, shopping, and many other activities, but we rarely find the time to renew our relationships with the people who are close to us, our family members, friends, and colleagues.

The practice of Beginning Anew is a practice of reconciliation. Beginning Anew can be practiced between two people or as a group. As one person speaks, the other person practices deep listening without interrupting, allowing the first person to speak from the depths of her heart.

In Beginning Anew we have three steps: sharing appreciation, expressing regret, and expressing hurt and difficulties. In the first step, sharing appreciation, we practice to recognize and acknowledge the positive attributes of the other person. Every one of us has both wholesome and unwholesome seeds. When we express our appreciation for the other person's positive qualities, we give him the opportunity to recognize the positive qualities in himself. At the same time, we water these very qualities in our own consciousness. For instance, perhaps our son is very kind and hardworking. He studies well and often helps us out. But once in a while he makes a mistake, and we correct him strongly right away. Yet because we have not told him how much we appreciate him, when we correct him, he hears only our criticism and blame. In this situation our relationship will be difficult. To improve the situation, we practice sharing our appreciation. If our son is doing well in school, we compliment him. We practice in the same way with our partner, husband, wife, friends, and other people in our life. We can share our appreciation with each other at any time.

The second step of Beginning Anew is expressing regret. We take this opportunity to share with the other person our regrets for the things we have done or said that might have caused him pain. This requires humility and the willingness to let go of our own pain and pride.

In the third step of Beginning Anew, we express our own hurt with mindful, loving speech, without blaming or criticizing. We speak in such a way that the other person can listen and receive our words. If we blame and condemn the other person, his heart will close and he will not be able to hear us. We ask the other person to help us to understand why he has spoken as he has, acted as he has to cause us so much pain. Perhaps at a later time he can share with us so that we can understand more deeply. If a strong emotion arises in us while we are expressing our suffering, we should simply stop and come back to our breathing until the emotion subsides. The other person can support us by following his breathing until we are ready to continue.

We can enjoy practicing Beginning Anew with our partner, our family, or our colleagues regularly. By doing this practice we will prevent small misunderstandings from accumulating. Rather, we will take care of them as they arise. At the same time, we cultivate our awareness and appreciation for the positive qualities our loved ones bring to our life. With understanding, all things become possible.

The Practice of the Wallet Reminder

When we are angry, we are not lucid. In that moment, we may say and do harmful things if we do not know how to practice mindfulness and protect ourselves and others. When we are hurt and overcome by our painful feeling, we are also not lucid. We have the tendency to blame and to condemn the person we think has hurt us.

But there are times when we are lucid and calm. We must take those opportunities to compose a peace note. We write on a piece of paper. "Dear one, I suffer and I want you to know it." We write these words down, and we slip the paper into our wallet. We are suffering, we feel hurt, but out of pride we don't want to tell our beloved one. We lock ourselves in our room and say, I don't need you, why should I need you? I am fine, don't bother me. But now we have already written our peace note: "Dear one, I suffer and I want you to know it." We write this peace note ahead of time so that when the time comes we can just pull it out and read it or we can simply hand it to our beloved one to read. We acknowledge our suffering and we open the door for communication, for peace and reconciliation.

On another piece of paper we write: "Dear one, I am doing my best. Please help." We keep this piece of paper in our wallet. When we are carried away by our anger, by our irritation, we can pull this piece of paper out and read it to ourselves and to the one we are angry at. It means, I am aware of my anger. I am doing my best to practice, to calm myself, to embrace my anger, and to look deeply into the roots of my anger. I don't want to speak or act out of my anger and irritation, and I need your support, I need your help. These are words of love. These are words of peace.

These practices are not difficult, yet even when we are aware of them, we may not remember to do them. For instance, if you have a difficult relationship with your mother, in the time that you are lucid and calm you can write a peace note to yourself: "My mother is a good woman. She has compassion and love in her, yet sometimes she becomes unpleasant and difficult to deal with. I have to help her in these moments rather than hate or punish her." As a daughter, son, or partner, each of us can write a peace note like this from our heart and keep it in our wallet. Then, in difficult moments, we can use the Wallet Reminder as a bell of mindfulness, to keep love and compassion alive in us and to help us refrain from uttering condemning and harsh words and from acting out of our anger and irritation.

If you know there are times when you are rough with your child, you can write down something similar and give it to your child: "My dear son, I don't want you to suffer, but there are moments when I am less than myself and irritated and difficult to deal with. Please be compassionate and patient, help me instead of hating me." Every one of us is capable of writing such sentences appropriate to our situation, when we are in a lucid state of mind, free from anger, because there are times when everyone manifests the seed of enlightenment, the flower of compassion. Just because you are the parent and he is your child, please do not think that it is unnecessary for you to write such things, that you are above such an exercise. These words you write down are the voice of your deepest love and caring. It is the voice of the Buddha or the voice of God in you that dictates these sentences.

You are your best when you write such loving sentences. When you are angry or narrow-minded, if your child or partner is a good practitioner, she will take out the piece of paper and read the lines you have written to her. When you see her doing this, you will know that she is practicing. If you are also a good practitioner, you will stop what you are doing, return to yourself, and take care of your strong emotions. As partners or as parent and child, you will be practicing together. You may also practice this with friends and colleagues. When you practice this way in times of conflict, it is a real victory, not only for you but for everyone.

Family Altars

Many people today, even people who have a partner or are part of an extended family, feel isolated and lonely. These people do not communicate what is in their hearts to those who love them. It is important that we create occasions for our family to come together and overcome the loneliness of modern society. When we restore our connections, our traditions, and learn from our past, we become more rooted.

In Vietnam, every home has an ancestral altar. On the anniversary of important events, such as the passing away of their father or mother, the entire family comes together at the house of the eldest child. This tradition is still alive in Vietnam, and everyone, including children, participates. It is a special opportunity to be with each other as one big family, to spend time together, to share a joyful meal and remember our loved ones.

For many of us who live in the West, it would be beneficial and enjoyable to adopt the practice of remembering our ancestors and receiving their support. A family altar may not be appropriate, although displaying family pictures or a family tree that shows the generations of our lineage can be a pleasant practice. To honor and remember our ancestors, we can place flowers in a vase or mementos near their pictures. When we gather as a family, on the anniversary of our grandmother's birthday or any other holiday, we can recall the beautiful qualities of our grandmother, of our grandfather. We name the positive contributions our grandmother has made. She was kind and loving to everyone. Grandfather was generous. He helped many people. Father was honest and hardworking and sacrificed so much to support his children and parents. We recall these beautiful qualities in our ancestors, and at the same time we nourish ourselves and our children by seeing that these characteristics are also in ourselves. When we connect to our ancestors in this way we feel stronger, with more courage to face the difficulties in our lives.

Getting Rooted

In Plum Village, we regularly practice the Five Touchings of the Earth to connect with our blood and spiritual ancestors. We draw on their strengths and ask for protection and guidance. Doing this practice helps us feel rooted and transforms our feelings of isolation and loneliness. We generally do it once a week to nourish our stability.

The Five Touchings of the Earth

I. In gratitude, I bow to all generations of ancestors in my blood family.

[Bell, touch the earth]

I see my mother and father, whose blood, flesh, and vitality are circulating in my own veins and nourishing every cell in me. Through them, I see my four grandparents. Their expectations, experiences, and wisdom have been transmitted from so many generations of ancestors. I carry in me the life, blood, experience, wisdom, happiness, and sorrow of all generations. The suffering and all the elements that need to be transformed, I am practicing to transform. I open my heart, flesh, and bones to receive the energy of insight, love, and experience transmitted to me by all my ancestors. I see my roots in my father, mother, grandfathers, grandmothers, and all my ancestors. I know I am only the continuation of this ancestral lineage. Please support, protect, and transmit to me your energy. I know wherever children and grandchildren are, ancestors are there, also. I know that parents always love and support their children and grandchildren, although they are not always able to express that love skillfully because of difficulties they themselves encountered. I see that my ancestors tried to build a way of life based on gratitude, joy, confidence, respect, and loving-kindness. As a continuation of my ancestors, I bow deeply and allow their energy to flow through me. I ask my ancestors for their support, protection, and strength.

[Three breaths]
[Bell, stand up]

II. In gratitude, I bow to all generations of ancestors in my spiritual family.

[Bell, touch the earth]

I see in myself my teachers, the ones who show me the way of love and understanding, the way to breathe, smile, forgive, and live deeply in the present moment. I see through my teachers all teachers over many generations and traditions, going back to the ones who began my spiritual family thousands of years ago. I see the Buddha or Christ or the patriarchs and matriarchs as my teachers, and also as my spiritual ancestors. I see that their energy and that of many generations of teachers has entered me and is creating peace, joy, understanding, and loving-kindness in me. I know that the energy of these teachers has deeply transformed the world. Without all these spiritual ancestors, I would not know the way to practice to bring peace and happiness into my life and into the lives of my family and society. I open my heart and my body to receive the energy of understanding, loving-kindness, and protection from the Awakened Ones, their teachings, and the community of practice over many generations. I am their continuation. I ask these spiritual ancestors to transmit to me their infinite source of energy, peace, stability, understanding, and love. I vow to practice to transform the suffering in myself and the world, and to transmit their energy to future generations of practitioners. My spiritual ancestors may have had their own difficulties and not always been able to transmit the teachings, but I accept them as they are.

[Three breaths]
[Bell, stand up]

III. In gratitude, I bow to this land and all of the ancestors who made it available.

[Bell, touch the earth]

I see that I am whole, protected, and nourished by this land and all of the living beings that have been here and made life easy and possible for me through all their efforts. I see all those known and unknown. I see all those who have made this country a refuge for people of so many origins and colors, by their talent, perseverance, and love—those who have worked hard to build schools, hospitals, bridges, and roads, to protect human rights, to develop science and technology, and to fight for freedom and social justice. I see myself touching my ancestors who have lived on this land for such a long time and known the ways to live in peace and harmony with nature, protecting the mountains, forests, animals, vegetation, and minerals of this land. I feel the energy of this land penetrating my body and soul, supporting and accepting me. I vow to cultivate and maintain this energy and transmit it to future generations. I vow to contribute my part in transforming the violence, hatred, and delusion that still lie deep in the collective consciousness of this society so that future generations will have more safety, joy, and peace. I ask this land for its protection and support.

[Three breaths]
[Bell, stand up]

IV. In gratitude and compassion, I bow down and transmit my energy to those I love.

[Bell, touch the earth]

All the energy I have received I now want to transmit to my father, my mother, everyone I love, and all who have suffered and worried because of me and for my sake. I know I have not been mindful enough in my daily life. I also know that those who love me have had their own difficulties. They have suffered because they were not lucky enough to have an environment that encouraged their full development. I transmit my energy to my mother, my father, my brothers, my sisters, my beloved ones, my husband, my wife, my daughter, and my son, so their pain will be relieved, so they can smile and feel the joy of being alive. I want all of them to be healthy and joyful. I know that when they are happy, I will also be happy. I no longer feel resentment toward any of them. I pray that all ancestors in my blood and spiritual families will focus their energies on each of them, to protect and support them. I know that I am not separate from them. I am one with those I love.

[Three breaths]
[Bell, stand up]

V. In understanding and compassion, I bow down to reconcile myself with all those who have made me suffer.

[Bell, touch the earth]

I open my heart and send forth my energy of love and understanding to everyone who has made me suffer, to those who have destroyed much of my life and the lives of those I love. I know now that these people have themselves undergone a lot of suffering and that their hearts are overloaded with pain, anger, and hatred. I know that anyone who suffers that much will make those around him or her suffer. I know these people may have been unlucky, never having the chance to be cared for and loved. Life and society have dealt them so many hardships. They have been wronged and abused. They have not been guided in the path of mindful living. They have accumulated wrong perceptions about life, about me, and about us. They have wronged us and the people we love. I pray to my ancestors in my blood and spiritual families to channel to these persons who have made us suffer the energy of love and protection, so that their hearts will be able to receive the nectar of love and blossom like a flower. I pray that they can be transformed to experience the joy of living, so that they will not continue to make themselves and others suffer. I see their suffering and do not want to hold any feelings of hatred or anger in myself toward them. I do not want them to suffer. I channel my energy of love and understanding to them and ask all my ancestors to help them.

[Three breaths]
[Two bells, stand up]

Using the Mind of Love

If you do not know how to take care of yourself and take care of
the violence in you, then you will not be able to take care of others. You must have love and patience before you can listen to your
partner or child. If you are irritated, you cannot listen; you have
to know how to breathe mindfully, embrace your irritation, and
transform it. Offer only understanding and compassion to your
partner and child—this is the true practice of love.

To take care of your partner and child, you need to learn to
take care of the child inside of you. Because you are so busy, you
have not had time to return to yourself and acknowledge the
presence of the wounded, neglected child within you. Go back to
this inner child; talk to her with all your compassion: "Darling, I
know you are there. We have suffered a lot. I have neglected you
because I have been so busy. Now I am home and I will take good
care of you." You must acknowledge and embrace your past
wounds and transform them nonviolently with mindfulness. You
must help these inner wounds heal through your attention to
them. In this way your inner child can grow and mature into a
caring, spiritual adult.

Your inner child is also interconnected with your son or
daughter. The Buddha said, "This is like this, because that is like
that." By taking care of one, you take care of the other. Your
partner has to do the same. When you know how to take care of
the wounded little girl in you, you can help take care of the
wounded little boy in him. This is truly worthwhile. What is the
use of having twenty-four hours a day if we do not do this? We
must use our time to heal the wounded child in us and in our

beloved one, because if we do not, we will not be able to raise our son or daughter in the way we should. The first step is to listen to the child within you and within your partner.

Having Respect for Mind and Body

Respect is essential in any relationship. We must respect the other person's body and mind. If there are things she does not want to talk about, we should refrain from asking about them. Even when relating to little children, we have to be respectful. A child has his own sorrow and pain. We have to respect this and not make fun of it. We cannot intrude into the secret zones of his heart. This would not be polite or kind. In fact, it would be a form of violence to do so.

Each one of us has painful memories that we do not want other people to know about. Understanding this, we should not intrude into someone else's forbidden cities unless she opens them up and invites us in. When she believes and trusts in us as a friend, she herself will open this door to us. Only then can we enter; otherwise, we have to remain on the outside and be patient.

In the teachings of the Buddha, body and mind are not separate, they are one. Respect for our mind implies respect for our body and vice versa. When you respect someone, not only do you respect his mind but you also respect his body. Someone can pat us on our shoulder, but there are areas of our body that no one has the right to touch. In Asia, many people consider the head a sacred part of the body. It is considered to be the altar of their ancestors. Out of respect, you are not allowed to touch someone else's head unless he is a child. When you have a relationship with someone, respect her body, because there are also forbidden zones in her body. Not only must you respect her heart, her consciousness, and her mind but you must also respect her body, because body and mind are one. Respect is very important in the teachings of all cultures.

You do not need to touch another person with your hands to cause hurt. The way you look, speak, and act can be considered a form of abuse. In our society, such abuse happens daily to children and adults alike, because we have not learned the way of respect.

One Year of Spiritual Service for Couples

To engage in a deep commitment, such as marriage, it is necessary to have a spiritual practice. When you get married, it is possible that you will create suffering for yourself and your partner. Within you are both positive and negative seeds, which you have received from your parents, grandparents, and all your ancestors. If you do not know how to recognize your negative seeds and you allow them to be watered, you, your partner, and your children will suffer. The happiness of many people is at stake. Children should not have to grow up in an atmosphere of tension and stress. You should have children only if your partner and you can live in harmony together. Getting married and having a family is dangerous if you are not prepared.

In Plum Village, we encourage couples to practice mindfulness for one year before getting married so they learn how to take care of themselves. If you know how to take care of yourself, you will be able to take care of your partner. You will know what to do and what not to do to keep your partner happy. We should set up practice centers that can serve as "Institutes for the Happiness of One Person," where everyone can go to get training. Here you would learn to make at least one other person, namely your partner, happy. During this year of practice at the institute, you would train yourself in the art of selective watering. You would water only the positive seeds and refrain from watering the negative seeds in yourself and in the other person. After one year, you could receive a certificate that entitles you to get married.

This is not a new idea. It has been practiced in many Buddhist countries. For instance, in Thailand it is a tradition for every young man to practice in a Buddhist temple for one year before he is entitled to get married. It is not military service but spiritual service. Even the son of the king has to do this kind of service. If the prince does not practice as a monk for one year, not only can he not be married but he is not entitled to become king. Spiritual service and training for young men and women can also be applied in the West. In a practice center or Institute for the Happiness of One Person, you do not need to shave your head and become a monk or nun. You need only to learn the practice of mindfulness. After one year of such training, you will be qualified to get married without the danger of doing violence to each other.

Keeping Respect Alive

In Plum Village, every time there is a wedding ceremony, we remind the couple-to-be to practice respect. Couples have to respect each other because respect is the foundation of love. The moment you begin to lose respect for the other person, you begin to lose your love. Therefore, during the ceremony the bride and bridegroom practice bowing to each other. In their own words, they promise, "Darling, I vow to respect you. Just because I am your husband or your wife does not mean that I can do anything I want. Anything I do to you that is disrespectful is a violation of my commitment. I understand that, without respect, I will not be able to nurture our love." Please, for your own sake, live and behave in such a way that your beloved one continues throughout your life to be your angel.

In a monastic community, we try to live and practice so that our brothers and sisters will always be the angels we need. We know we should be the continuations of the Buddha for one another. Just because someone is our student or younger sister or brother does not mean that we can behave with anything less than full respect. As monks and nuns, we practice the Mindfulness Trainings because respect is our foundation.

Peace Treaty for Couples

Between many couples there is tremendous conflict, but even in the most difficult of relationships there are occasional moments of harmony and joy. During these times of togetherness, we usually want to avoid bringing up painful matters. Because we bury these issues, however, our problems just come up again and again, each time worse than before. We have to make good use of those moments when we are calm, loving, and caring. These are the times when we should sign a peace treaty. We can go to our partner and say in our sweetest voice, "My dear one, I treasure our moments of love and affection together. I hope that we have many more moments like this. Can we do something to make them happen more often? Can we prevent difficult situations from arising and destroying us? In the name of our love, our commitment to each other and our children, can we agree to sign this treaty of peace to take care of our anger?"

You may want to adapt the wording to your particular situation, discuss the treaty with other family members, and even hang it up where the whole family can see it. It is a promise to practice peace for your welfare, your partner's, and your children's. It offers many concrete suggestions that can help you take good care of our anger and irritation. It is a wonderful document.

A Peace Treaty for Couples

In order that we may live peacefully and happily together, in order that we may continually develop and deepen our love and understanding, We, the undersigned, vow to observe and practice the following:

I, the one who is angry, agree to

1. Refrain from saying or doing anything that might cause further damage or escalate the anger.
2. Practice mindful breathing and return to myself to take care of my anger.
3. Calmly, within twenty-four hours, tell the one who has made me angry about my anger and suffering, either verbally or by delivering a peace note that uses loving speech in writing what I have to say.

against adults and children is a heavy burden on society. Many families have been broken by sexual misconduct. Children who grow up in such families may suffer their entire lives, but if they get an opportunity to practice, they can transform their suffering. Otherwise, when they grow up, they may follow in the footsteps of their parents and cause more suffering, especially to those they love.

We know that the more one engages in sexual misconduct, the more one suffers. We must come together as families to find ways to protect our young people and help them live a civilized life. We need to show our young people that happiness is possible without harmful sexual conduct. Teenage pregnancy is a tragic problem. Teens are not yet mature enough to understand that with love comes responsibility. When a thirteen- or fourteen-year-old boy and girl come together for sexual intercourse, they are just following their natural instincts. When a girl gets pregnant and gives birth at such a young age, her parents also suffer greatly. Public schools throughout the United States have nurseries where babies are cared for while their mothers are in the classroom. The young father and mother do not even know yet how to take care of themselves—how can they take care of another human being? It takes years of maturing to become ready to be a parent.

The Third Mindfulness Training helps us to be civilized and responsible in our relationships. We become "aware of the suffering caused by sexual misconduct." To make young people, adults, and society aware of this suffering, we should get together and invite people to share their own life experiences. When we are aware of the suffering, we "vow to cultivate responsibility."

4. Either verbally or by note ask for an appointment later in the week, like Friday evening, to discuss this matter more thoroughly.

5. Not deny or suppress my feelings, and not say: "I'm not angry, it's fine, I am not suffering. There's nothing to be angry about."

6. Look deeply into my daily life—while I am sitting, standing, walking, or lying down—in order to see
   - How I myself have been unskillful at times.
   - How I have hurt the other person because of my own unmindful habits.
   - How the strong seed of anger in me is the primary cause of my anger.
   - How the other person is only the secondary cause.
   - How the other person is only seeking relief from his or her suffering.
   - That as long as the other person suffers, I cannot be truly happy.

7. Apologize immediately, without waiting for the Friday appointment, as soon as I recognize my unskillfulness and lack of mindfulness.

8. Postpone the Friday meeting if I do not yet feel calm enough to meet with the other person.

I, the one who has made the other angry, agree to

1. Respect the other person's feelings, not ridicule him or her, and allow him or her enough time to calm down.

2. Not press for an immediate discussion.

3. Confirm the other person's request for a meeting, either verbally or by note, and assure him or her that I will be there.
4. Practice mindful breathing and deep looking to see how
   - I have seeds of anger and unkindness in me that make the other person unhappy.
   - I have mistakenly thought that making the other person suffer would relieve my own suffering.
   - I make myself suffer when I make him or her suffer.
5. Apologize as soon as I realize my unskillfulness and lack of mindfulness, without making any attempt to justify myself and without waiting for the Friday meeting.

We vow with all our heart and in the mindful presence of the family and sangha to abide by these articles and to practice wholeheartedly. We ask that they help to protect us and grant us clarity and confidence.

Signed, _____,
_____,

the _____ Day of _____, in the Year _____, at
_____.

Mindful Protection of Yourself and Your Relationships

To better understand the practice of protection, please study the Five Mindfulness Trainings in Chapter 3, particularly the third,

sexual responsibility. By practicing the Third Mindfulness Training, we protect ourselves, our family, and society. In addition, by observing all the trainings we learn to eat in moderation, to work mindfully, and to organize our daily life so we are there for others. This can bring us great happiness and restore our peace and balance.

Expressing Sexual Feelings with Love and Compassion

Animals automatically follow their instincts, but humans are different. We do not need to satisfy our cravings the way animals do. We can decide that we will have sex only with love. In this way we can cultivate the deepest love, harmony, and nonviolence. For humans, to engage only in nonviolent sexuality means to have respect for each other. The sexual act can be a sacred expression of love and responsibility.

The Third Mindfulness Training teaches us that the physical expression of love can be beautiful and transcendent. If you have a sexual relationship without love and caring, you create suffering for both yourself and your partner, as well as for your family and our entire society. In a culture of peace and nonviolence, civilized sexual behavior is an important protection. Such love is not sheer craving for sex, it is true love and understanding.

Respecting Our Commitments

To engage in a sexual act without understanding or compassion is to act with violence. It is an act against civilization. Many people do not know how to handle their bodies or their feelings. They do not realize that an act of only a few minutes can destroy the life of another person. Sexual exploitation and abuse commit

You cannot be called a civilized person if you do not act in a responsible way. To be responsible means to love. "I protect you because I love you. I refrain from doing certain things because they would destroy both of us. I will honor the Mindfulness Trainings, and I don't need to struggle, because I really love you. I want you to be happy, so I have to protect us both." This is love. When you just satisfy your animal needs, it is not love—it is destruction. In the past you may have been destructive, harming yourself and the other person, and you may now know what it means to suffer. Above all, to be happy means to be free. This is why we vow "to learn ways to protect the safety and integrity of individuals, couples, families, and society."

In the Third Mindfulness Training, we are also "determined not to engage in sexual relations without love and a long-term commitment." We vow, "To preserve the happiness of others and myself, I am determined to respect my commitments and the commitments of others. I will do everything in my power to protect children from sexual abuse and to prevent couples and families from being broken by sexual misconduct." It is the right medicine for our time.

When we vote for members of Congress, parliament, or city hall, remember that we have the right to find out whether the candidates practice the essence of the Third Mindfulness Training and can truly represent us. We have a right to know. If they do not respect their family commitments, act irresponsibly, and destroy their own families, how can they represent us in government? We should consider not only their words but also the way they live their lives. We should vote only for candidates who live according to the principles of civilization and nonviolence.

As individuals, as couples, as families, and as a society, we can recite the Five Mindfulness Trainings and discuss how to live according to this ideal of protection and healing so that we honor our commitments. Practicing the Third Mindfulness Training is a concrete way to cultivate nonviolence.

CHAPTER SIX

To Love Means to Be Truly Present

Practicing Peace with Your Child

A child is a great responsibility whether you are rich or poor. Your child is an extension of yourself, a continuation of your blood and your spirit. If you have children, please remember that the environment in which children grow up affects them greatly. If you are going to practice peace, you must do something to make the world a better environment for your child and for all children.

One of the most important things you can do is establish peace between yourself and your partner. Children feel helpless in an atmosphere of conflict. Even if parents do not say or do anything explicitly violent, when there is no harmony between them, the child sees this. Children are extremely sensitive to their parents' hidden emotions and suffer because they have no power to alter the situation.

In the past, when people lived in rural communities with extended families, if a stormy atmosphere arose in the family, a child could escape to the land, to a garden or pond, taking refuge in nature and other life; the trees, the fish, and the birds. He could go to his uncle's or aunt's house to take refuge in another "mother" or "father" who would help restore his joy. Today, most people live in nuclear families with only a mother, father, and one or two children; they no longer live in homes that house three or four generations and other people to whom children can go for comfort. When their parents are at war with each other, children have no one else to turn to. Without an escape, violence can invade their inner lives.

As adults, we need to practice mindfulness ourselves, and we need to help our children become mindful. We need to teach them self-protection and care, and we need to teach them to grow and flower in their natural compassion for others. The best way to support our children in developing mindfulness is for us to live mindfully. By observing us, our children will learn the same habit. If we are always absent, our children will not profit from our example. Too often, when we are at home we are not really present. We may be preoccupied by problems at the office. Our body is present, but our mind is elsewhere. When you realize this has happened, you can practice mindful breathing to help you come back to yourself, and you can tell your child, "My dear, I am really here for you."

When you practice mindful breathing, it is not difficult to be there for the people you love. Simply bringing your awareness to your in and out breaths allows your body and mind to become one. Then you will be well established in the here and now. You will be able to offer your beloved one the most precious gift, your own true presence.

When you make breakfast, when you eat, drink, or clean the table, you can practice being truly present, for yourself and your loved ones. When you do the dishes after dinner, practice mindful breathing so the time of dish washing together becomes pleasant and meaningful. Do not feel you have to rush so you can sit down and enjoy your coffee afterward. If you hurry, you waste precious time, the time for being alive. When you establish your true presence, you can bloom like a flower during your daily activities. When your child sees you practicing like this, she will learn to do the same. Later she will be able to create happiness for herself and her children.

ORANGE MEDITATION

An easy way to teach your child to practice is to eat an orange in mindfulness with him. Usually, we are not mindful and get lost in thinking, forgetting ourselves, forgetting the orange. We worry about our projects and become overwhelmed, possessed by thoughts about the past and the future. Take time together to eat an orange mindfully. You need only fifteen minutes. Sit in a relaxed way, hold the orange in your hand, look at it, and smile so that you and your child become real, become fully present. By doing this, you also make the orange become fully present. If you are really there, the orange will reveal itself as a miracle, because the orange is nothing less than a true miracle. You can visualize it: the orange tree gave birth to a tiny flower. With the nourishment of the sun and the rain, a tiny fruit was born from this flower. The earth, the sky, and the whole cosmos came together so that this orange could grow into a beautiful fruit. Now the orange is in your hand. It is a real miracle. You too are a miracle. The encounter between two miracles is true life.

Children enjoy this orange meditation very much and through it begin to live each minute of life in mindfulness. It also teaches them concentration, which is the source of understanding and wisdom. Living in mindfulness and concentration, they will have more understanding of others and know what to do to help and what to avoid in order not to cause more suffering.

The Breathing Room

Every family should have a peaceful space or breathing room, where any member can take refuge. In this new century, it is time for everyone to have a true refuge. It is important to have a place to recuperate, to restore one's peace and stability. When the United Nations was established in New York, it was clear that a spiritual center was needed within the building, so the Church Center for the United Nations was built. In this center is a small meditation room. Though it does not have a cross or a Buddha statue, it is a place where people go to take refuge and return to themselves, in silence.

A breathing room does not need to be large. It can even be part of another room. It can be a closet you have emptied and cleaned that has room to sit comfortably and breathe. We simply need a place to go when we do not feel solid and peaceful. We have rooms for eating, for guests, for television and Ping-Pong, for everything except peace. I would like to see territories of peace set aside in schools, hospitals, city halls, corporate offices, and prisons—areas that no one can violate.

The breathing room in your home should be a territory where everyone has immunity, where anyone will be protected and safe. You can design it according to your needs; it does not have to be Buddhist, Christian, Jewish, or anything else. In this room you might have flowers, a few cushions, and a small bell. Invite your children to help set up the room, and show them how to use it. When you or your partner is angry or unstable, the room is there for you; you can go there right away to restore yourself. When someone takes refuge in this room, everyone else should turn off the television and respect his or her need for peace and quiet. To establish this as a family practice, you might want the whole family to sign a treaty agreeing that the room or space will be used only for the restoration of peace and stability.

MAKE IT A GOOD DAY

You can make the breathing room a part of your daily life, not just a place of refuge during an emotional storm. Each morning, before leaving home, you and your child can share a few minutes of mindful breathing. You can make it a habit: instead of just wishing each other a good day, you actually make it so, by starting your day this way. Walk quietly together into the room, sound the bell three times, and come back to yourselves. With this practice, the day always begins well.

In the evening, before going to sleep, your child can also visit the breathing room, sound the bell, and breathe mindfully. Even if it is not your bedtime, please join her in the breathing room and then accompany her to her bedroom. Afterward, you can continue what you were doing. Just before you retire to your own bed, go yourself to the breathing room and practice sitting, listening to the bell, and smiling. This practice supports you and your child in making the day end peacefully and will help the next day begin peacefully.

Calming a Family Storm in the Breathing Room

If, in spite of your peace treaty, tension arises between you and your partner, your child should be able to escape. She needs only to say, "I am going to the breathing room." Please consider this a bell of mindfulness, helping you to become aware of what you are doing to your child or partner. Support your child by stopping whatever you are saying or doing; bring your attention to your breathing and your need to restore your peace. Do this out of love for your child because you do not want to transmit violence to her.

It is best if you can say right away, "I'll go there, too, my dear, I'll join you." You can take her hand and practice walking slowly, breathing in and out, together. Show her that you are copractitioners of peace. Mindfully open the door and enter the breathing room with her. Then you and your child sit down and practice sounding and listening to the bell. A few minutes of mindful breathing can make a big difference.

Sometimes you may not be capable of joining your child as soon as she goes to the breathing room. You might be angry and upset and choose to continue your work in anger. If you are cooking dinner, for instance, you might discover that you are cutting the carrots without joy, transmitting and expressing your violence by your act of cutting. But then, when you hear your child sound the bell in the breathing room, it reminds you to go back to your breathing, to calm yourself. Suddenly your movements become more peaceful, and the carrots suffer less. You may think, Preparing dinner is important, but supporting my child is even more important. You put your knife down and do walking meditation to the breathing room. You enter gently, sit close to your child, and practice breathing in and out with her. This is a great support—this is love.

Your child will feel comforted because her mother supports her, and she will feel inspired because her mother has transformed. When your partner sees you practicing, he too will begin to feel differently. You and your child have become bells of mindfulness for him. A few minutes later, he may join you in the breathing room. Together, the three of you breathe mindfully and embrace your difficult emotions.

This is the most beautiful thing that can happen in the life of a family. It is the cultivation of peace, nonviolence, and love. You may have millions of dollars or a van Gogh painting on your living room wall, but they are not as precious and beautiful as you and your child sitting together, practicing peace.

Investing Yourself in Your Child

Organize your family life so your child feels at home and embraced by the love of his parents, brothers, and sisters. Be a friend to his friends; participate as much as you can in his life. If you like to watch television with your child, choose one good program to watch together, sharing your joy and excitement. Also educate him about programs that are harmful, that can water the seeds of violence, hatred, and fear in him. If you do not do things together, you cannot educate your child.

Skillful Means

Sometimes, when trying to alleviate a loved one's suffering, a bodhisattva pretends to do things she does not normally do. This requires skillful means. A bodhisattva will go fishing if the person she wants to help goes fishing. She might not really want to catch fish but only to be with the one who needs her support. Or she may sit in a bar with others who are drinking. She sits there not to drink but only to help people who are drowning themselves in alcohol. This is the practice of skillful means. You do things together with your child in order to orient and guide him in the right direction.

The time you spend with your child is an investment in the future. Your main task is to raise her in such a way that a future will be possible. You are your child, and he is your continuation. If he has no future, you have no future. As a teacher, I feel the same way about my students; if they have no future, I have no future. The time I spend with them is a good investment for society and for the world. We must try to transmit the best of ourselves to our students and our children.

Arrange your daily life in a way that gives you the time to invest in your children. If you are cut off from them, you cannot be happy. If parents and children cannot communicate, problems arise. Your life reveals its true meaning when you transmit the best of yourself to your children. Therefore, investing time, energy, and love is your main task as a parent, and when you can join together with your partner in this investment, you will become true companions.

Parents are like the first leaves of a banana tree; their task is to nourish and bring up the younger leaves. Chasing after fame, money, and sex becomes less important when we are motivated by a noble desire. Giving ourselves to our children, students, and society brings us true happiness.

Aim to be an orange tree that does its best to offer blossoms and beautiful fruit. This is an act of love. Who says an orange tree does not love? She knows perfectly well what love is. Every day she is in touch with the sunshine, the rain, the air, and the soil to nourish what is best in her: the leaves, blossoms, oranges, and the seeds within each orange. Like the orange tree, animals also know how to love, teaching their young ones to run, to fly, and to find food. They know how to care for them. By investing in our children every day, every night, and every hour, we can do the same.

Deep Listening and Loving Speech in the Family

We all have wounds inside our hearts, and we all need someone who can listen mindfully to understand our suffering. Children especially need to be listened to and understood. You have to inquire into both their well-being and their difficulties. Respect their hurt and vulnerabilities. As a parent, you are their first teacher and doctor, supporter, comforter, and defender. You are a bodhisattva for your child, always seeking to alleviate her suffering. You do not have to be a Buddhist to practice this way. Everyone can practice being present and listening deeply, whether Muslim, Jewish, Christian, Buddhist, or of no religious faith.

Deep listening and the Five Mindfulness Trainings are ways out of inner violence and outer conflict for individuals and families. We can use the trainings with our families to water the seeds of compassion and love within each of us and to cease watering the seeds of violence and anger. We can use them in our schools and communities to build a peaceful world.

When you practice listening, you can sit with each other and speak from your experience. Share with your family how deep listening and loving speech have helped you in your daily life and how the Five Mindfulness Trainings have helped you. We can also learn a lot from thoughtful exchanges with other families and friends: how to prevent violence from entering our minds and hearts, how to keep it from taking root and growing, how to transform arrows into flowers. Learning from others' experience spreads the influence of nonviolence.

Listening to Heal Your Child's Suffering

It is important that you sit down and listen to your children with concentration, and understand their difficulties and pain. If they are wounded, you have to know, and you have to give them as much time and energy as possible. Find a way to speak to your child so that she feels embraced by your caring and concern. Talk to her in a way that gives her the confidence and courage to tell you what is happening in her life. She may be suffering in school or in relationships with friends. She may be verbally or physically abused, lonely or depressed and afraid to tell you, so you have to create the kind of relationship that allows her to be honest. Encourage her to tell you the truth. Help her speak out about her suffering, and try your best to give counsel.

Take time to listen to your child, take time to love. Listening to understand your child's suffering is the true practice of love. Providing necessities like food, clothing, and medicine is not the only way to show your love. Even more important is giving your time and opening your heart to listen.

Listening and helping to heal suffering is the practice of peace, is the practice of love. Loving is the most important thing we can do. Of course we are busy, but are we so busy that we cannot love? We take the time to read a novel or a magazine, time to watch television or talk on the phone, but we do not take time for each other. Set aside the time to listen.

Be available for your child when he comes to you. You should be there one hundred percent. Your mantra, your motto, is "My dear, I am here for you one hundred percent." Mindfulness enables you to do this. It is not easy to do if you do not practice mindfulness, if you allow yourself to be possessed by your worries and your projects. If you cannot be there for your child when he needs you, then you are still his physical father or mother but not really a father or mother in full, because you are otherwise occupied, absorbed in your thinking, concerns, and work. This is why it is important that you make yourself available with the practice of mindful breathing. Learn to be in the present moment for your children.

If you have not yet practiced deep listening with your child, now is the time to begin. This should be the practice of all members of your family. You should say, "My dear, I understand your difficulty, I understand your suffering. I will do my best to support you." We have to listen with care in order to know how to water the good seeds in our children and keep them from suffering themselves or causing additional suffering.

After you have learned your child's suffering, give her your support and advice, using kind words. Later you may need to take compassionate action on her behalf. You may have to go to your child's school, for instance, or talk to other parents. This too is the practice of love.

Sometimes, we are so full of irritation and anger that we are unable to listen to our children. At times like this, we must bring awareness to these feelings and allow ourselves to return to ourselves. We have to stop, pay attention, breathe, and transform anger into compassion. When compassion is born in our heart, we will feel fresh and loving, and then we will know that we are ready to listen.

Everyone has difficult moments and should have time alone to work them out. Even though your child needs you to listen, if you are not prepared, you have to ask him to wait. You can say, "Darling, I am just not fresh enough to listen to you right now. Please allow me a few hours." Your loved one will understand.

In the same way, if your child is not yet ready to share what is happening inside her, you have to offer your love and presence and be willing to wait. You can say, "It's okay. You don't have to speak about it now. I am ready to listen whenever you want to share. I know that you suffer and can't tell me today, but you may feel like telling me later. I care about you very much; we will sit together and help you suffer less." Your child needs you to be there in this way. No one else in the world may be able to offer this kind of presence. You are acting as a bodhisattva of deep listening, someone who is able to be truly present for others.

Helping Your Child Speak Peacefully

Sometimes your child has so much suffering inside that he thinks he can express his feelings only loudly and angrily. In these moments, you also have to help him. You can say, "My dear, I am ready to listen to you, I have all the time in the world to listen, but please breathe first, then calmly tell me everything." This is the art of loving speech. Both parents and children have the capacity to express themselves lovingly. All of us can do this with some practice. It is also important that you help your child express himself with peaceful language, because if your child cannot speak peacefully with you, then he will not be able do so with others.

Do not let your child drown in a crisis. If you practice breathing with your child right from the beginning of her life, you will know how to handle storms when they arise. Stay with your child when she is overwhelmed by strong emotions. Do not react or shout at her because she is upset. Instead show her how to breathe and how to walk and how to embrace her feelings. In the beginning, she may not be able to do these things by herself. However, as you continue to practice with her, she will learn to take care of her emotions on her own.

You have to help your child cultivate the art of deep listening and loving speech while she is young. If she learns to speak calmly with her teachers, fellow students, friends, and others, she will be able to offer her best insight in any situation. When both parents and children cultivate loving speech and deep listening, this is true peace education.

A commitment between you and your child is a peace treaty. If you do not abide by this peace treaty, how can you expect others to observe it? When you are carried away by your irritation and despair, you violate the peace treaty, and your child becomes the victim of your behavior. Honoring the treaty between you and your child is the practice of peace. It has everything to do with peace and nonviolence in the world.

Organizing Family Listening Sessions

The practice of deep listening and loving speech is the path to transforming the violence and conflict between parents and children. These methods can help keep communication open and can reopen communication when it has become difficult or blocked.

In hour-long family listening sessions, everyone has a chance to be heard. During the first session, however, no one may be ready to talk, so your family may benefit from the presence of someone from outside the family, someone who is respected by all. A third party can bring stability and safety, allowing a parent, spouse, or child to listen and communicate better. Sometimes it is necessary to engage a professional therapist to help the family, but you must be sure that the therapist will listen deeply—your healing depends on it. If the therapist can truly listen, everyone will suffer less after only an hour of talking. But you can do the same thing in the context of your family with no outside assistance. For love to be reborn, we have to learn again how to listen to one another.

A Peace Treaty to Protect the Family

You can make a pact with your partner: "My dear, we must protect our child. Every time anger or violent language is about to break out, we have to be aware of it. We should not express our aggression in her presence. Let us come together for her sake, for the sake of the future. Let us sign a treaty and agree that in the presence of our child we will not fight. Every time war between us is about to break out, we will remind each other that our child is present." We can signal each other with a word like "Peace" or a sign, like clasped hands and bowed head, that will make us stop and breathe.

This is something everyone can practice. Many parents take care not to make noise when their child is sleeping; they know how to move about the house silently so they do not wake up their child. Protecting your child from violence is a similar practice. Every time violence is about to arise, you have to be careful and do something. Practice mindful breathing, and remember what you promised: "My child is here. I have to protect her by not allowing the violence in me to erupt."

You can add another clause to the peace treaty: "Every time we feel the energy of anger or violence arise, we have to practice mindful breathing, walking, and looking deeply into our anger."

Children as Family Peacemakers

In Plum Village in France, we use the monastery bell, the clock chime, and the first three rings of the phone as bells of mindfulness. When we hear the sound of the bell, we stop whatever we are thinking, saying, or doing in order to be aware of our in and out breaths. The bell of mindfulness gives us a chance to relax our body and return to ourselves. We once more become aware of the many wonders of life that are present for us and enjoy the fact that we are alive. Breathing in and out three times, we restore our calm and peace. We become free. We stop and breathe, not with solemnity or stiffness but with joy. Our work becomes more rewarding, and we are fully in touch with the people around us.

When there is a storm in the house, your child is quite capable of sounding the bell for the whole family. This can be part of your peace treaty. If the child sounds the bell, the parents have to stop, quit their arguing, and come back to their breathing. The child is acting as a bodhisattva, an enlightened being. Parents can be bodhisattvas as well and sound the bell to calm the atmosphere. All family members can support one another in this way.

I know a family in Switzerland with seven or eight children. All of them enjoyed the practice of mindfulness when they stayed in Plum Village. When they returned to Switzerland, they were able to keep peace and harmony among themselves for several months. However, over time the practice became thinner and thinner, weaker and weaker. One day the youngest child, who was six years old, heard a dispute among her older brothers and sisters. Everyone was shouting loudly at the same time; this had not happened since their time in Plum Village. Frustrated, she took the small bell from the table and rang it. Everyone stopped to breathe and then burst out laughing. The atmosphere was completely changed.

The Cake in the Refrigerator

Another simple peace practice for children is what I like to call the cake in the refrigerator. When a child sees his parents quarreling, and if there is no bell in the house, he can just touch his mother's hand and say, "Mommy, I think there is a cake in the refrigerator." You, as his mother, will understand that this is his way of saying, "Mother, I suffer; I cannot stand this." The cake, whether it is in the refrigerator or not, is always there for him to use. You will smile and say, "This is true, my dear, just go to the backyard and arrange the table and chairs. Mommy will go to the kitchen to take out the cake and make some drinks for us all to enjoy." This gives both you and your child an escape. Your son can immediately run to the backyard, breathing room, or other peace space, and you can go to the kitchen. Your child has stopped the war.

Do not worry if there is no cake. You can always quickly prepare something, perhaps juice or tea. You have reestablished peace in the family. This is a skillful practice that can be initiated by a child, a simple way children can help end conflict between parents.

I have offered many retreats in which young people have come to practice, even though their parents were not interested. During the retreats, the young people began to realize that their parents also suffered. Often parents want to stop the violence in their homes but cannot because of their pride. After they returned home from retreats, the children practiced diligently to relieve the heaviness and suffering in their families. Eventually, their parents also began to practice. Children and young people can initiate actions of peace and create an atmosphere of harmony in the family.

Family Meals in Mindfulness

One of the best practices for creating peace in the family, regardless of religion or culture, is sharing a meal together mindfully. In the past, it was common for families to bow their heads before eating and say grace, giving thanks for the food before them. During those moments they felt a real sense of togetherness. People were aware that they were a family sitting around a table. You do not need to be religious to feel this sense of gratitude and togetherness. As long as you find something beautiful, good, and true to believe in and abide by, you have the equivalent of God in your life. It is already wonderful that you are sitting around the table breathing in and out mindfully, smiling and feeling together as a family.

In Plum Village, we recite the Five Contemplations before each meal to nourish our gratitude and to nurture our mindfulness as we eat. It is a practice similar to saying grace. At home, when the whole family eats together, you can invite your children to read the Five Contemplations aloud. In the first contemplation, we are reminded, "This food is the gift of the whole universe: the Earth, the sky, and much loving work," and in the second we ask, "May we live and eat in mindfulness so that we are worthy to receive this food." It is not difficult to be worthy to receive the food. We need only to be fully present and enjoy eating mindfully. When we eat while we are angry, forgetful, or irritated, thinking of things other than the meal and our family, we do not appreciate the gift of food before us and act ungratefully. The next three contemplations are "May we transform our unskillful states of mind, and learn to eat in moderation. May we take only food that nourishes us and prevents illness. We accept this food in order to realize the way of understanding and love." During the recitation, everyone should look deeply into the food he or she is consuming, to see that the meal really nourishes his or her body and mind.

When we recite the Five Contemplations, we maintain mindfulness and the feeling of gratitude and togetherness as a family throughout the entire meal. This is the practice of nourishing peace in the family.

THE FIVE CONTEMPLATIONS

- This food is the gift of the whole universe: the Earth, the sky, and much loving work.
- May we live and eat in mindfulness so that we are worthy to receive this food.
- May we transform our unskillful states of mind, and learn to eat in moderation.
- May we take only food that nourishes us and prevents illness.
- We accept this food in order to realize the way of understanding and love.

Try to organize a family meal at least once a day. Sometimes this is difficult because our work prevents us from going home for meals, but we have to use our intelligence and make an effort. Try to plan your schedule so that you can retain the best of family life. Eating a meal together celebrates your togetherness as a family.

In Plum Village, we eat every meal together. It takes time for all of us to stand in line, serve our food, and walk slowly to our seats, but we wait for everyone to sit down before beginning the meal. We are not wasting time, because our practice is to enjoy every moment. Eating as a community, we foster a feeling of togetherness. It is nourishing to see the beautiful sangha around us, practicing as a family.

When we eat a meal together like this, we become fully present. As we serve ourselves, we breathe in and out, smile, and look at the food, aware of every movement we make. We enjoy ourselves, getting in touch with the flowers, trees, and birds singing outside. Every moment is joyful. At Plum Village, at the beginning of the meal we sit together in silence for about twenty minutes, avoiding any unmindful conversation that might chase away our feeling of togetherness.

Your family may like to try eating in silence, perhaps for only the first five minutes. Eating this way enables you to maintain awareness of the precious food you have before you and the wonderful presence of your family. After this period of silent eating, you will be calm and present. Your conversation will be more thoughtful, more likely to promote happiness and togetherness.

Other Mindful Family Practices

Doing Walking Meditation

Walking meditation is another important way to cultivate nonviolence within your family. To show your children how to enjoy walking meditation, you can practice as a family. Children catch on very quickly as to how walking can calm our feelings and help us recover our peace.

When you are angry or sad, you should stop what you are doing and walk mindfully to the breathing room. You will already feel better by the time you have arrived. When your child is upset and suffers, take her hand and invite her to do walking meditation. Take the hand of your partner or child, and show how he can walk to release his anger and pain. Teach him to enjoy walking meditation so he can calm negative feelings and get in touch with the positive elements within and around him.

Please remember not to force your child to do too much of any one practice at first. You may be able to enjoy walking for longer distances, but your child may have less concentration. If he is very young, he may feel comfortable walking mindfully for only five or ten steps. Afterward, allow him to run, then invite him to take another five or ten mindful steps before he runs again. In the beginning, he may need your guidance, but as he learns to enjoy this practice, he will be able to do it on his own.

Appreciating Nature

Walking together outdoors increases our happiness, peace, and harmony. A picnic with family and friends provides a wonderful opportunity to enjoy the beauty of nature. Nature is our mother, and if we are cut off from her, we will become sick. We have to learn how to live in harmony with nature and teach our children to do the same. For our own sake, we have to do everything we can to get in touch with nature and to protect our environment. There are small things we can do: We can contribute to the maintenance of public parks. We can go camping or hiking and visit wildlife preserves or national parks. We can carpool, cutting down on traffic and the use of fossil fuels. We can avoid using poisonous or harmful fertilizers and insecticides in our yards. We can study books that help us learn about nature. We can take away the fences between our backyards and, together with our neighbors, create a green zone behind our houses. These are just a few things we can do to reconnect with nature and protect her.

You can awaken your child's interest in nature by giving her some plants of her own. Plant a few trees in your yard or go to a plant nursery or flower shop together and choose some bulbs and small plants for indoors. Learn how to take care of them together. Learn how to make your plants happy, because your happiness depends on the happiness of your plants.

Watching Television Mindfully

Each family needs an intelligent policy concerning television. In most cases, it does not work just to forbid children to watch television. The family should come together to discuss how to promote peace at home and resolve any divisive issues.

Once I was invited to the home of a family in Boston. The grandmother of this family is very traditional and usually does not watch television. Occasionally, however, she likes to watch a film with her family. When she consents to watch a film, she is ready five minutes before it starts, dressed beautifully, as if she were going out to the cinema. Everyone joins her, also beautifully dressed, because they have decided to see the program together, as a family. The entire family goes to the cinema in their own living room.

As parents, we should explain to our children why we believe certain entertainment can be dangerous. Watching television, we can poison our consciousness with violence, hatred, and fear. Through our practice of the Fifth Mindfulness Training, on consumption, we protect ourselves and our children. Allow your children to ask questions and make decisions with you; they are intelligent enough to discuss and understand these issues.

You don't want your children to turn to television just to fill their time. We so often complain that we do not have enough time, yet when we do have fifteen minutes or an hour to ourselves, we often don't know what to do. Most of us cannot bear to feel lonely, so we pick up a novel or a magazine, or open the refrigerator, or talk on the phone to fill the vacuum. Consumption as a way to escape ourselves is a serious problem. You want your children to learn that every moment is precious and wonderful. Supervise what your children watch on television or the Internet, where they can potentially absorb countless toxins. Mindless consumption can destroy them. With freedom comes responsibility.

Commit yourself as a parent to consume intelligently, to consume only positive things. There are many healthy, refreshing, and healing elements inside us and around us. When we consume in a way that protects the healthy elements within us, we are protecting the healthy elements around us. This is a deep practice, the essence of the Fifth Mindfulness Training. Talk with your family about committing as a group to this way of peaceful living.

Practicing Deep Relaxation Together

You and your children need deep relaxation to overcome the stress of contemporary life. Your children need to learn to take care of themselves because school can be very stressful. You can teach deep relaxation to your children and offer to lead them in it every day, before eating dinner or going to sleep. After a while your child might decide that he wants to lead you in it. Fifteen or twenty minutes of deep relaxation, led by you or your child, will be precious time spent together.

Getting Children in Touch with Their Ancestors

You and your children can get in touch with your ancestors and heritage by making or working on a family altar or a peace altar for their room, or the breathing room, or the peace place. You can also make a family tree, so your children can see how they are connected to their ancestors, create a picture album of your grandparents and great-grandparents, or even arrange the pictures of your family to illustrate how your children are related to their ancestors. Tell your children your family's history. Such a conversation gives you an opportunity to talk about your roots and your children a chance to know their extended family.

Peace in Our Schools

Peace begins with you and your family; this is the foundation for everything else. The more stable and happy your family relations are, the more you can help others. Once you succeed in your home, you can reach out to your school. Collaboration between parents and schoolteachers will help protect your child; without this dialogue, your child cannot grow up the way you hope. You have to help teachers organize school as a family. When I was in school, a teacher was like a father or mother, big sister or big brother, and there was love and communication between a teacher and the students. School was a place where you learned how to live. Now, too often, it is only a place where you receive information or are put in danger. In too many schools, human relationships are no longer important and students no longer see themselves as brothers and sisters. This is a great loss.

Parents and other mindful people need to help our schoolteachers, who are often struggling in difficult circumstances. We have to reach out and help defuse the violence within teachers and students. Many teachers do not know how to handle difficult emotions in themselves, and every day these seeds are watered by the violence of their situation. Concerned parents can arrange meetings with other parents and schoolteachers to combine insights and practice. Perhaps we can organize retreats and discussions for schoolteachers to help them learn and practice ways to cultivate peace. Practice centers can offer Days of Mindfulness especially designed for schoolteachers. The environment of a practice center can be powerful and beneficial, but only if the practice center is itself organized as a family. Our active participation is the best way to take care of our children and transform our schools into peaceful places where students and teachers trust and respect each other. We can grow only in an atmosphere of trust and love.

Extending Peace Beyond the Family

Please let your children know that they are capable of loving and caring for other children, other living beings. As they grow up, they should know what is going on in the world. Many do know that they are fortunate and are grateful for what they have and for the peace in their lives. They are also aware that there are many children who must work hard day and night to earn a living, that there are children who die because they lack even the most basic food and medical care. Many children are aware that there are children whose lives are at risk every day from the threat of bombs and land mines, who are orphaned by wars and illness.

We can actualize our children's awareness by encouraging them to get involved, to join actions of peace. For example, we can ask them to spend less money on themselves and to contribute to buying medicine for poor children. Or they could sponsor an orphan in a far-off country who needs food and other basic necessities.

It is not only a matter of donating a few dollars a month: When giving, you open the door of your consciousness. Whether children live in New York, Los Angeles, London, or Paris, they can reach out and help. They can correspond with other children who are less fortunate than they. When we teach children concrete ways to help relieve the suffering of others, and when they are motivated by a desire to love and help, they become tiny bodhisattvas and are protected from the violence, hatred, and anger invading our society.

At first, it may be difficult for your child to have an interest in what is going on. But once the willingness is there, your child's compassion will blossom like a flower, and he will be eager to relieve the suffering of others. When you and your family are capable of offering a needy child a glass of soy milk, compassion is born in you and you begin to suffer less. You are happy and your life has more meaning. The whole family can participate in and benefit from this practice of peace and generosity.

We nourish and protect our children by our own practice. Everything we do—meditation, education, communication—should be done to understand more deeply and to give rise to the compassion within us. Our practice must be relevant to the needs of young people. We have to help them nourish their compassion, cultivate their awareness, and foster awakening in themselves. We must learn to take care of our young people and help them grow into tiny bodhisattvas. This is the best way to prevent violence from penetrating their hearts.

PROTECTING PEACE
COMMUNITY AND SANGHA PRACTICES

When I sit with my spiritual community, my sangha, I practice mindful breathing and am aware of the ancient bonds that tie me to my sangha. The Buddha founded the sangha 2,600 years ago. During all those years and in many different lands throughout the world, the sangha has brought understanding, stability, and joy. It continues to do so today.

As a member of the sangha, I am like a cell in a body. At the same time, I feel that I am the body, I am the sangha. The body is 2,600 years old, and therefore I feel that I am 2,600 years old as well. Though you may still be young, you are at the same time very old, because all of us are connected to generations of our ancestors and history, connected to their sorrows and joys, to their failures and their freedom. When you connect with a spiritual teacher or with your older brothers and sisters in the practice, you too become the sangha. Your spiritual community helps you become solid and wise. Through your teachers, you touch the many other ancestral teachers in your spiritual lineage.

Connecting with Our Blood and Spiritual Lineages

When I give a talk or transmit the Five Mindfulness Trainings, I breathe in and out mindfully and become aware that an individual, separate self is not the person who is giving the talk. It is not an individual who is transmitting the Mindfulness Trainings, because I am the sangha. Many generations of teachers are transmitting the practice through me, not me alone. If you look at me with attention, you will see my teachers in me, and their teachers inside them, all the way back to the Buddha. You will see the whole lineage of ancestral teachers transmitting the Mindfulness Trainings. Whatever I do, it is done by my whole lineage. When you are connected with your fellow practitioners and with your teacher, you are connected with all ancestral teachers and all practitioners as well.

By taking refuge in a spiritual community, you become rooted in the experience, wisdom, and consciousness of those who have gone before you. At the same time, you yourself become a perennial root for the flowering of all the young people who will continue after you. Your life becomes eternal. When I see a young person practicing mindful walking and breathing, I see myself in him, in her. I feel very youthful. I know that this person will continue the practice and will carry me into the future. I know that I will climb the hill of the twenty-first century with all of my students. Together, we will go through the next century. My life will continue because I am going as a sangha and not as an individual, separate self.

When you practice mindfulness, you also connect with your

own biological family, your brothers and sisters, your mother, father, and grandparents. Through them you connect with your whole lineage of blood ancestors. When you are disconnected from your biological or spiritual family, you become weak and easily lost. Your resolve of Right Action can evaporate like a drop of water. If you are estranged from your family, you must seek to reconnect with them. If you have a son or daughter from whom you are estranged, please try to connect with him or her. It is your children who will carry you into the future and allow you and your spirit to stay young. We must practice to overcome our difficulties with our children, and with our brothers and sisters. By protecting ourselves, we protect our parents and our family, and each of us can then help our loved ones transform negative seeds into positive ones. The support of family and community helps us be strong and handle our difficulties mindfully.

Great happiness comes from this practice. When you establish a connection with your ancestors, you will feel supported by them and by all the teachers in your spiritual tradition. With this awareness you become fearless, because you know that you are acting as a living tradition, a whole lineage. With this insight, death is defeated and you remain young forever. At the same time, you are as old as the sun and the moon.

Practice, the Hallmark of a True Sangha

To be a true spiritual community, a sangha, we do not have to be perfect. The sangha during the life of the Buddha was not perfect. This is very comforting to know. As humans, we all have our weaknesses, but this does not prevent us from being a true sangha. Any sangha that makes a sincere effort to practice and bring forth the positive seeds in its members is a true sangha.

If negative seeds such as jealousy or discrimination come to the foreground, then as brothers and sisters in the practice we should help each other to recognize them, to smile at them and, with loving-kindness, invite the positive seeds to replace them. We must do this without blame or condemnation. We should remember that we are all only humans trying our best to practice. From time to time, violence and anger may manifest in our fellow practitioners, but our practice is to smile and embrace them.

Freedom from the Prison of Self

The second half of the twentieth century was characterized by individualism, the desire to do things only for the sake of our separate self. Our society has been dominated by the desire for fame and wealth, material things, and hedonism. As a result, many people have fallen away from their spiritual traditions and their families. We cannot have healthy families and communicate if we believe joy can be found only in the pursuit of power, sex, and wealth. Happiness does not come from consumption of things.

Tragically, people in the Third World are imitating the materialism of the West. In China, Vietnam, and other countries, many have abandoned their spiritual traditions. They long to buy the latest, most sophisticated video equipment, portable telephones, color televisions, and other technological toys. Consumption has become the focus of their lives. Many people no longer believe in anything, no longer have ideals; they no longer have a cause to serve.

We need to look deeply to see what we are now doing with our lives. We let individualism prevail in the twentieth century, and frankly, we have made a mess of it. We must begin anew for the twenty-first century; we need a new, different direction. We can no longer continue destroying ourselves and the planet we live on. With determination we can abandon the cult of individualism and the self, and act and live in harmony, in the spirit of interbeing.

The sangha, the spiritual community, is our new direction, and sangha building is the noblest task we have before us. To build a sangha, we have to learn to open ourselves to each other and to share our experiences, insights, time, and love. The sangha must be the refuge for us all in this new century.

Living the Insight of Non-Self

Neuroscientists who study the brain have discovered, as we have in meditation practice, that there is no single self. The human brain is made up of billions of brain cells, neurons, each communicating with billions of other neurons. There is no CEO, no director, no boss operating the brain, yet perfect harmony reigns. When scientists look into the way neurons act, they see the neurons communicating ceaselessly with one another. Each neuron fires electrical impulses to other neurons at the speed of 250 miles per hour, and in a fraction of a second, it fires again.

Communication is continuous; there is constant sending and re-ceiving. The neurons live and work together as a community in harmony.

The cells in our body do not act out of duty or obligation; they simply operate together as a sangha. The lungs are doing their best to renew the blood through the intake of oxygen. The lungs do not say, "You, the blood, you need me in order to be red and oxygenated. You have to be grateful to me." The lungs never think this way. It is their pleasure to breathe in and out and to offer oxygen to the blood cells. The blood cells travel to all the other cells in our body, to release oxygen and other nutrients. They never say, "We travel so much just to bring you oxygen. You should be grateful to us. We have done too much; now it's time for us to retire." They never say things like this. A blood cell just enjoys doing what it has to do for the benefit of the whole body. There is no discrimination in our body. If you are a scientist ob-serving how the human body functions, you will see that all ele-ments of the body are operating in accordance with the insight of non-self. All the cells of our body contain the wisdom of nondis-crimination; all live together as a sangha.

When you observe a beehive, you see the same thing. No boss is directing anything. No bee says to another, "You, Bee Number One, you have to do this for me, and you, Bee Number Two, you have to go in that direction to get pollen for me." There is no di-rector at all. The queen bee is not directing; she is not a queen in the sense of giving orders or governing. Her duty as a queen bee is to produce the eggs, the next generation of bees. Even without a director in the beehive, every bee acts in perfect coordination with every other. Bees do not need to tell each other what to do.

The way they live their daily life, the way they act, is their message. They communicate through the way they do things. Sometimes a bee goes back to the hive and begins to dance. With its dance, the bee indicates to other bees where they can find pollen.

This kind of harmony exists among other social insects as well. Termites engage in the same sort of well-organized team- work. These communities function with intelligence and wis- dom. No one gives any orders, and communication flows. Scientists have observed that the chemicals exuding from each bee serve as a means of communication. All the bees are continually ready to receive information from each other and respond to it and act in a flawless way. No bee needs to tell another how to behave.

Although many scientists have witnessed this reality of non- self in the human body and in nature, very few have made use of this insight in their own lives. Nuclear scientists, neuroscientists, biologists, sociologists, and psychologists—they have all seen the truth of non-self. They write and speak about it, but for the most part are unable to live according to it. Many scientists, when they leave their workplace, go home and continue to live as separate selves, behaving with their families and friends as if they had never seen the reality of the insight of non-self.

Many spiritual practitioners behave in the same way. We lis- ten and learn about the teachings of non-self and interconnect- edness, and yet, when we go back home to our partners, our parents, our brothers and sisters, we do not apply the insight of non-self. We still get angry and jealous, bound as we are by our small self, incapable of behaving like the bees, the neurons, and the cells in our body. To help us break free from this habit, we have to practice with a sangha. If we rely on the sangha, the sangha will be there for us. To be good sangha builders, we must recognize the truth of non-self and of interbeing, and find ways to implement this insight in the daily life of our community. We cannot be satisfied with just the insight of non-self; we must live it.

Cultivating the Insight of Interconnectedness

To build community, it is important to accept the insight of interbeing, of interconnectedness. We must realize that happiness is not an individual matter. Finding happiness through our separate, individual self is impossible.

The family is a sangha, society is a sangha, and the Earth and all life are a sangha; this is why we have to learn to live as a sangha, not only with other human beings but with other species as well. We have to accept animals, plants, and minerals as our partners, as members of our community.

As we cultivate and keep alive the insight of non-self and interconnectedness in our daily life, we free ourselves from the prison of individualism. We open our eyes to the reality that the happiness of our family and the larger community is also our own happiness. With this insight we will no longer feel separate and we will know how to behave in a way that brings harmony and happiness to our family, our society, and our mother Earth.

We have been imprisoned for so long and have suffered so much from our individualistic way of living. Our practice for the

new century should be to transform the notion that we are separate selves and to liberate ourselves from the prison of the individual. The most meaningful practice we have today is to learn
how to live as a sangha.

The Sangha River

If we are a drop of water and we try to get to the ocean as only an
individual drop, we will surely evaporate along the way. To arrive
at the ocean, you must go as a river. The sangha is your river. In
our daily practice, we learn how to be a part of this river. We learn
how to look with sangha eyes, how to walk with sangha feet, how to
feel with a sangha heart. We have to train ourselves to see the happiness of our community as our own happiness and to see the difficulties of our community as our own difficulties. Once we are
able to do this, we will suffer much less. We will feel stronger and
more joyful. As members of a sangha, we can develop our individual talent and our individual potential, and at the same time
contribute to and participate in the talent and happiness of the
entire group. Nothing is lost; everyone wins. A sangha has the
power to protect and carry us, especially in difficult times. We
have a better chance to develop our potential and protect ourselves when we participate in the work of sangha building.

The Sangha River is a community of friends who practice the
way of harmony, awareness, and compassion. In the sangha we
practice mindful walking and breathing. The sangha radiates a
collective energy that can support us and make us strong. The
sangha is a boat that transports us and prevents us from sinking
into the ocean of suffering. This is why it is so important that we
take refuge in the sangha. Allow your community to hold you, to

transport you. When you do, you will feel more solid and stable and will not risk drowning in your suffering. Taking refuge in a sangha is not a matter of belief. "I take refuge in the Sangha" is not a statement of faith; it is a practice. As a river, all the individual drops of water arrive together at the ocean.

Practice Centers Offer Protection

In daily life there is a lot of danger. During as little as a half hour in a city, for instance, multitudes of toxic images and sounds enter your senses. A practice center offers true refuge. In a practice center you can restore your balance very quickly.

Children and young people generally do not live in practice centers or monasteries, and their environments can be highly toxic. What they see, hear, and touch every day can water the seeds of violence and their animal nature. This is why establishing a peace place or breathing room in your home is so important for you and your children. The sangha, too, can help you create peace places for children and families.

As a mindfulness practitioner and a sangha member, you can influence other parents and show them ways to protect their children from their anger. You are a sangha for them, helping nonviolence take root in their families. You can teach both mother and father to sit and listen compassionately to each other and to practice loving speech. You can teach them mindful breathing and walking for inner peace. You may begin with the intention to protect the children, but soon you find yourself embracing the entire family. With skillful means, you can intervene in any situation. This is engaged practice.

The sangha can also offer protection to couples. As a layperson, you are exposed to many temptations. Without a sangha to protect you, you may suffer from inner conflict and the desires of your animal nature. The sangha helps you remember your Buddha nature. The sangha helps people handle their sexual energy and honor their commitments, strengthening the bonds of marriage.

In a spiritual community, you have plenty of opportunities to serve within and outside the sangha, to help people suffer less, to make them smile again. You can practice loving everyone as your brother or sister. You can study and live in accordance with the teachings and express yourself in the language of love and understanding. When inappropriate sexual energy arises, you can transform it into other kinds of energy, like the energy to study, to practice, or to work. According to Vietnamese wisdom, the most difficult form of practice is lay practice. Living in a temple is more supportive, because even if you stray one step, a brother or a sister will be there to help. A sangha can help you in the same way.

It may seem that in living an individual, separate life you are freer than when you are involved in a community, but this freedom can be a disguise for being lost. When you are caught up in desires, you lose all your freedom, and freedom is the very foundation of happiness. When you get entangled in an inappropriate love affair, you are no longer free and you suffer very much. You also make other people and your sangha suffer. The loss of freedom is the loss of happiness.

Sanghas Relieve Suffering

In Plum Village, we do our best not to be trapped in our own small world. Although we take care of the daily needs of our community—engaging in working meditation, hosting retreats, and many other activities—we remain in touch with the suffering of the children everywhere in the world, and this connection helps us to stay healthy.

Plum Village sponsors schools in Vietnam where children learn to read and write and at lunchtime are offered a meal which includes a glass of soy milk. Many of these children come from poor families and suffer from a lack of protein.

One day I was looking at a picture of children from Ha Trung village, the village where my mother was born and raised. When I looked deeply and mindfully at the faces of the little girls in the village, I saw each one as my mother. My mother was exactly like them, nourished with the same kind of food, accustomed to the same kind of climate.

If a young girl in this village does not receive a glass of milk each day, she may grow up and give birth to an undernourished boy. I did not have enough protein growing up. If I had, I might be taller than I am now. If you want to take care of me, then you must take care of the little girl in the picture. You must make sure that every child in the village has a glass of soy milk for lunch.

When people come into contact with a sangha, they have a chance to get in touch with the reality of the world. In doing so, their seeds of compassion and loving-kindness will be touched. Everyone comes with pain inside. The sangha not only helps them embrace their suffering but also helps nourish their seeds of compassion and understanding. They suffer much less when they allow these positive seeds to be watered. It is important, when we touch suffering, to preserve our own peace. In order not to be overwhelmed, discouraged, or pessimistic, we must balance the suffering we touch by nourishing our stability and happiness. The awareness of happiness and the awareness of suffering can nourish each other. If we practice looking deeply at our pain and our happiness, we will realize that happiness and suffering are interdependent and can only be understood in relationship to each other. The sangha gives us a chance to participate in its work of love. While we are helping the community, we are also helping ourselves.

We must not neglect the practice of love and compassion. We have to care for the children and all the people of the world as well as those who are part of our sangha. We should not spend all our time on our own concerns. We must allow a few doors and windows to be open to the suffering of the world. This is for our own sake.

Inclusiveness and Compassion

As a sangha, we train ourselves in the practice of inclusiveness. We know that everyone suffers, even those who have tried to hurt us. As a living continuation of Jesus Christ, of Muhammed, of Moses, of the Buddha, and of all spiritual ancestors, you have to help everyone. If you practice inclusiveness, discrimination and anger will not arise in you, even in times of great pain.

Without mindfulness and concentration, we cannot understand the reality of what is. If we open the door of reality, we can show others its true nature. What exactly is reality? The suffering of everyone is reality. Rich and poor, North and South, black, yellow, red, and white is reality. Our daily consumption of poisons and our weapons industry are reality. Our lack of time and energy for ourselves and others is reality. The destruction of human life, of other species, and of the environment by our un-mindful way of living—these are reality. If we want a future for our children and our children's children, we need to take the time to look deeply into the true nature of reality. Deep looking will bring about insight, and with insight we can act.

Please do not think that God is on your side alone. God does not take sides. God is compassion and inclusiveness. If God loves everyone, how can we exclude anyone? We say God bless America, but we must add God bless everyone, because everyone is a child of God. Do not believe that by eliminating the other you can find peace. Helping them is the *only* way.

CHAPTER EIGHT

A CALL FOR GREAT
COMPASSION

A traditional Vietnamese Zen garden is very different from a Japanese Zen garden. Our Zen gardens, called *hon non bo*, are wild and exuberant, more playful than the formal Japanese gardens with their restrained patterns. Vietnamese Zen gardens are seriously unserious. For us, the whole world is contained in this peaceful place. All activities of life unfold in true peace in the garden: in one part, children will be playing, and in another part, some elderly men will be having a chess game; couples are walking; families are having picnics; animals are free to wander around. Beautiful trees are growing next to abundant grasses and flowers. There is water, and there are rock formations. All ecologies are represented in this one microecology without discrimination. It is a miniature, peaceful world. It is a beautiful living metaphor for what a new global ethic could bring.

War is not a necessary condition of life. The root of war, as with all conflicts, is ignorance, ignorance of the inherent goodness—the Buddha nature—in every human being. The potential for ignorance lives in all of us; it gives rise to misunderstanding, which can lead to violent thoughts and behavior. Although ignorance and violence may not have manifested in your life, when conditions are sufficient, they can. This is why we all have to be very careful not to water these seeds and not to allow them to develop roots and grow into arrows.

The Roots of War

When one country attacks another, it is out of great fear and a kind of collective ignorance. For instance, the French fought to keep Vietnam as their colony, because they thought that, if they possessed Vietnam, they would be happy. So they sent many young men to Vietnam to kill and to be killed. We know, when we look deeply, that happiness does not come from possessing something or someone, it comes from kindness and compassion, from helping to ease suffering.

If the American people had sat down and practiced looking deeply, they would have seen that the Vietnam War was entirely unnecessary, that their own lives could not be improved through the suffering of another country or the suffering of their own young men. The United States senselessly wasted many lives in this war when it could have supported both North and South Vietnam in their different models of development, helping the Communists and the non-Communists alike to rebuild their societies. This would have been much wiser than supporting one side and fighting the other. If France and the United States had yielded autonomy to Vietnam, Laos, Cambodia, and Thailand, helping these countries to develop instead of waging war, all sides would have profited from such a friendly relationship. After a long period of suffering, these countries are finally moving in this direction, but this could have happened much earlier without the terrible loss of life.

All violence is injustice. We should not inflict that injustice on ourselves or on other people. Historians and teachers as well as politicians should look deeply at the suffering caused by wars, not just at the justifications that governments give for them. We have to teach our children the truth about war so they learn from our experiences and understand that violence and war are not the right way, they are not the right actions to take. We have to show our children that people on both sides of war—the French and American soldiers in Vietnam as well as the Vietnamese people— were victims of the ignorance and violence rooted in their societies and governments. Remember, there were no winners.

As long as we allow hatred to grow in us, we continue to make ourselves and others suffer. As we look deeply at the wars in our recent history, we have to transform our hatred and misunderstanding into compassion. We have to recognize that those who have made us suffer are also victims. Many who had a father, brother, or friend killed in the Vietnam War have been able to transcend their suffering and to reconcile with the other side, Vietnamese and American. They have done this for their own sake and for the sake of their children.

How can we as individuals influence the collective consciousness of our nations and move in the direction of peace? We do this by uprooting the roots of violence and war within ourselves.

To prevent war, we cultivate nonviolence. We practice mindfulness in our daily life so that we can recognize and transform the poisons within us and our nation. When we practice nonviolence in our daily life, we see the positive effects on our families, society, and government.

Peace Is Possible

In the summer of 2001 in Plum Village, about eighteen hundred people came and practiced with us. Among them were a few dozen Palestinians and Israelis. We sponsored these people hoping they could have the opportunity to practice walking meditation together, to share a meal together, to listen to the teachings of mindfulness practice, and to learn the act of deep listening and gentle, loving speech. The Israelis and Palestinians spent two weeks with us and participated in all activities.

At the end of their stay, the whole community gathered together and our visitors stood up and gave a report. After only two weeks of practice, they had transformed very deeply. They had become a community of brothers and sisters, Palestinians and Israelis. They said to us, "Dear community, dear Thay, when we first came to Plum Village we couldn't believe it. Plum Village did not look real to us because it is so peaceful. In Plum Village, we did not feel the kind of anger, tension, and fear that we feel constantly in the Middle East. People look at each other with kind eyes, they speak to each other lovingly. There is peace, there is communication, and there is brotherhood and sisterhood." One member of the delegation said, "Thay, we spent two weeks in paradise." Another person wrote to me after he returned home and said, "Thay, this is the first time that I have believed that peace is possible in the Middle East."

What did we do to make the Third Noble Truth—well-being and peace are possible—real to them? Honestly, we did not do much. We just embraced these friends from the Middle East as brothers and sisters. They learned to walk mindfully with us; to breathe in and out mindfully with us; to stop and to be there in the present moment with us, and to get in touch with what is pleasant, nourishing, and healing around them and within themselves. The practice is very simple, but supported by a practicing sangha, they were able to succeed more quickly than on their own and to touch the peace and happiness within each of them.

Together we all followed the basic practice: to do everything mindfully. We establish ourselves in the here and now in order to touch life deeply. We practice mindfulness while we breathe and walk and talk and brush our teeth and chop vegetables for meals and wash dishes. That is the basic daily practice that our friends learned. We in the sangha offered our support, sitting with our visitors and practicing listening with compassion with them.

We trained them to speak in such a way that the other side could hear and understand and accept. They spoke in a calm way, not condemning anyone, not judging anyone. They told the other side of all the suffering that had happened to them and their children, to their societies. They all had the chance to speak of their fear, anger, hatred, and despair. Many felt for the first time that they were listened to and that they were being understood, which relieved a lot of suffering within them. We listened deeply, opening our hearts with the intention to help them express and heal themselves.

Two weeks of the practice of deep listening and using loving speech brought a lot of joy to our visitors and to all of us in Plum Village. We were reminded, hearing these stories, that during the Vietnam War we Vietnamese, too, had suffered terribly. Yet our practice allowed us then and allows us still to see that our world is beautiful, with all the wonders of life available every day. This is why we know that our friends from the Middle East, too, can practice in the middle of war around them.

There were moments during the war when we wished so hard that there would be a cease-fire for just twenty-four hours. We thought that if we had only twenty-four hours of peace, we would have been able to breathe in and out and smile to the flowers and the blue sky. But we did manage to breathe in and out and smile, even then, because even the flowers had the courage to bloom in the middle of war. Yet still, we wanted twenty-four hours of peace during the war. We wanted the bombs to stop falling on us.

During the war in Vietnam, young people came to me and asked, "Thay, do you think there will be an end to the war?" I could not answer them right away. I practiced mindful breathing, in and out. After a long time I looked at them and said, "My dear friends, the Buddha said everything is impermanent, including war."

Before going back to the Middle East, our friends promised us that they would continue the practice. They told us that on the local level they would organize weekly meetings so they could continue to walk together, sit and breathe together, share a meal together, and listen to each other. Every month they have had an event to do this. They practice true peace even in the midst of war.

True Peace Negotiations

When you come to any negotiation, whether at work or in a meeting with other parents, teachers, or neighbors, you have hope for peace. When your representatives go to a negotiation table, they hope for peace. But if you and they do not master the art of deep listening and loving speech, it is very difficult to move toward peace in any situation or to get concrete results. If we have not transformed our inner block of suffering, hatred, and fear, it will prevent us from communicating, understanding, and making peace.

I beg the nations and governments who would like to bring peace to the Middle East and other countries to pay attention to this fact. We need our governments to organize peace negotiations so that they will be fruitful. A very important factor for success is creating a setting where true communication can be practiced, where deep listening and gentle, loving speech can occur. It may take one month or two just for people to learn how to listen to each other, to talk so that the other side can hear and understand. It is important not to be in a hurry to reach a conclusion or an agreement about what to do for peace to be possible. One month or two is nothing compared with years of pain and suffering. But if we have a great determination, then five days may be enough to restore communication between people. Two weeks were enough for our Palestinian friends and our Israeli friends to begin to understand and to accept each other as brothers and sisters, to begin to practice and create peace. Two weeks were enough for them to have hope.

Too often in the past, peace conferences have been environments where people came and fought each other, not with weapons but with their fear. When we are carried away by our fear and prejudices, we cannot listen to others. We cannot just bring two sides together around a table to discuss peace when they are still filled with anger, hatred, and hurt. If you cannot recognize your fear and anger, if you do not know how to calm yourself, how can you sit at a peace table with your enemy? Facing your enemy across a table, you will only continue to fight. Unable to understand yourself, you will only continue to fight. Unable to understand yourself, you will be unable to understand the other person.

The secret of creating peace is that when you listen to another person you have only one purpose: to offer him an opportunity to empty his heart. If you are able to keep that awareness and compassion alive in you, then you can sit for one hour and listen even if the other person's speech contains a lot of wrong perceptions, condemnations, and bitterness. You can continue to listen because you are already protected by the nectar of compassion in your own heart. If you do not practice mindful breathing in order to keep that compassion alive, however, you can lose your own peace. Irritation and anger will come up, and the other person will notice and will not be able to continue. Keeping your awareness keeps you safe.

Peace conferences must create environments that can help people calm down and see that they are suffering and that the other side is suffering also. Many leaders have tried to sponsor talks and discussion, but theirs was not the way of practice. They did not practice to transform anger and fear into deep listening and loving speech. When leaders do practice, there will be a chance for true reconciliation. After the practices of deep listening and kind and loving speech have dissolved bitterness, fear, and prejudice, people can begin to communicate with each other. Then, reaching peace will be much easier. Peace will become a reality.

Creating Peace in Government

In 1997 I went to India and had the opportunity to meet with the vice president of India and president of the Parliament, Mr. K. R. Narayanan. Our discussion took place on the opening day of the budget session of the parliament, just before three new members of the government were to be sworn into office. I thanked Mr. Narayanan for taking the time to meet with me on such a busy day. He replied that, busy or not, it was always important to him to meet with a spiritual person. We sat together and discussed how the chairman and members of parliament could apply the practice of mindfulness, deep listening, and loving speech in the congress. I suggested, "Mr. Narayanan, maybe it would be good to begin every session with the practice of mindful breathing. Then, a few lines could be read to bring awareness into everyone's mind, such as: 'Dear Colleagues, the people who have elected us expect that we will communicate with each other using kind and respectful speech and deep listening in order to share our insight so that the parliament can make the best decisions for the benefit of the nation and the people.' It would take less than one minute to read such a text, and afterward something like the bell of mindfulness could be used.

"Every time the debate became too hot, and people were insulting and condemning each other, the chairperson could sound the bell of mindfulness, saying, 'We are not calm enough, please let us stop arguing and be silent for one or two minutes.' Then he could invite everyone to breathe in and out—breathing in calming, breathing out smiling—until the atmosphere became calm. Then the one who was speaking would be invited to continue his or her speech."

Mr. Narayanan was very attentive to what I said and invited me to come back and address the Indian parliament on that issue. Ten days later I was leading a retreat in Madras, and someone showed me a newspaper article reporting that the chairman had set up a committee on ethics for the parliament with the task of improving the quality of their communication.

This kind of practice of nonviolence is possible everywhere, in every country. We urgently need to reduce the animosity and tension in government. If there is an atmosphere of harmony, calm, and sharing in government, there will be a future for our country and for every country.

We are not helpless. We have to do our best, we have to stop the war inside ourselves. This is the practice of peace, and it can be done every moment. If we do not practice peace in our lives, war will continue to break out within us and around us.

Electing Peaceful Politicians

Our Congress, like a family or a community, should itself promote peaceful engagement with its members. When we elect people to Congress, we invest our hope and trust in them and expect them to listen to other members. All members of Congress should have the capacity to listen, to realize what is good, intelligent, and valuable. Too often they are not listening to their colleagues; they are listening just to their own ideas or thinking about how they are going to disagree and argue as soon as the other person from the other party stops talking.

We do not elect representatives to Congress only to fight. We elect them with the expectation that they will be able to combine their wisdom, experience, and insight with that of other members of Congress. We expect them to use calm speech, to listen, to learn from others, and to incorporate their ideas into the insights of others. Unfortunately, they do not say to us, "If elected, I will practice deep listening in order to profit from the insight of other members of Congress." As voters, we have to ask them, "Are you willing to practice listening deeply to your fellow members once you are elected? If not, we are not going to vote for you." We have to insist that politicians run their campaigns in a way that aids us in making better decisions. When we vote without demanding that they use deep listening and loving speech, the result is too much anger and division in Congress—a kind of war in our national family.

I personally would like to vote for representatives who have the capacity to listen and speak mindfully. I think we all might want to write our senators and representatives to recommend that they consider practicing deep listening and loving speech. We could suggest that in the Senate and the House of Representatives there be a committee on compassionate listening and speech.

We also need Congress to pass concrete laws that protect us

and our children from violence and toxic influences. Our representatives make many promises, but we must demand more than promises. In certain Asian countries, for instance, the distribution of pornographic materials is not allowed. Television programs that stimulate sexual desire are banned. In this respect, the young people there are better protected. Similarly, some European countries refuse to import American films that are explicitly pornographic or too violent. This has been done in other countries without the loss of freedom or civil rights.

We must wake up and put our awakening into practice, asking for action when we elect members to Congress.

Establishing a Council of Sages

I propose that the people of the United States ask Congress to form a Council of Sages that can listen deeply to people who feel they are victims of discrimination, exploitation, and social injustice. America is suffering greatly. The destiny of a nation is too important to leave to politicians alone.

The First Noble Truth of Buddhism is the recognition of suffering, or ill being. The first step in curing ill being is to understand the situation and find its roots. This is the practice recommended by the Buddha. Members of the Council of Sages would have the duty of inviting people who suffer to speak out. They would have the responsibility of listening deeply to them.

Setting an Example for Other Nations

If America truly listens to the suffering of her own people, this will inspire great respect in other countries, and perhaps the citizens of other lands will think, "Maybe we can do the same." There is suffering in our country also, and we can follow America's example and listen to and understand the suffering of our own people. America can be a role model for the world, but only if America can practice listening to herself. This would be her most beautiful export. God will indeed bless an America capable of doing this. I believe America can realize the great potential of doing this Right Action of peace for herself and the world.

The best protection for any country is to practice compassion and understanding toward other nations. Yet not many countries practice this. If we want to have lasting peace between nations, we should help other countries to live in peace as well. The stability of other countries guarantees our own stability. Though it is logical, many powerful countries do not see this truth and continue to live off the weaknesses of poorer countries. The developed countries of the North cannot be safe if the developing countries of the South are being destroyed. The survival of the North depends on the survival of the South. Therefore, the best protection for the North is to help protect the South. If the North continues to exploit the labor and the resources of the South, sooner or later the North will collapse. This is the teaching of interbeing; it is the practice of nonviolence and peace based on the insight of interbeing.

The first step toward peace is to listen to and understand yourself and your fellow citizens. Otherwise, how can you listen to and understand the suffering of other people? How can you understand the suffering of Afghanistan, Israel, Palestine, or Iraq? Awareness of suffering is the First Noble Truth. All people suffer from the same things: social injustice, discrimination, fear, and fanaticism.

Fundamentalism is very much alive in countries around the world, and in America also. Many people believe they alone are on the side of God and behave as if they are God's only children and the lives of others are not as precious. We all want God to bless our country and our people. But to say about the other, "Everything they do is evil; everything we do is good," is the root of wrong actions. When we think in this way, we are not seeing others' value; we are acting out of ignorance and misunderstanding, without compassion for others' suffering and fears. This is why all our actions must be based first on the act of understanding. After beginning again the work of removing misperceptions, injustice, inequality, and discrimination inside our nation, we will be in a position to help the world.

Practicing Deep Listening with Other Countries

If America invests all her heart and mind into this practice, then other people will also be able to tell her about their suffering. If America goes back to herself and restores the spirit of her forefathers, America will be truly great. She will then be in a position to help other countries establish similar forums, to invite other groups and countries to express themselves.

The setting must be one of safety and love. Countries from around the world can come together not as enemies that bomb and destroy each other but as wise people sponsoring sessions of deep listening. All nations could come and help with the practice; people from different cultures and civilizations would have the opportunity to speak to one another as fellow human beings who inhabit the same planet. In addition, people who are not just politically minded but humanists who understand the suffering of others could be invited—people who know how to sit and listen calmly, with compassion. These people would know how to create an atmosphere of peace without fear so that others can have the chance, the inspiration, and the desire to speak. We must be patient. The process of learning about each other's suffering will take time.

If such an international forum were broadcast around the world, everyone could participate and have the chance to learn about the causes of suffering. The First and Second Noble Truths of the Buddha, the awareness of suffering and the awareness of the causes of suffering, could be practiced together by billions of people.

The First and Second Noble Truths will lead us to the Third and Fourth Noble Truths, namely the awareness that there is a path out of suffering and that that path consists of certain concrete steps, such as Right Understanding, Right Thinking, Right Speech, and Right Action.

Creating Peace in the World

The antidote to violence and hatred is compassion. There is no other medicine. Unfortunately, compassion is not available in drugstores. You have to generate the nectar of compassion in your heart. The teaching of the Buddha gives us the means to generate the energy of compassion. If we are too busy, if we are carried away every day by our projects, our uncertainty, our craving, how can we have the time to stop and look deeply into the situation—our own situation, the situation of our beloved one, the situation of our family and of our community, and the situation of our nation and of the other nations? Looking deeply, we find out that not only do we suffer but also the other person suffers deeply. Not only our group suffers but the other group also suffers. Once awareness is born, we know that punishment, violence, and war are not the answer.

The one who wants to punish is inhabited by violence. The one who endures the suffering of the other person is also inhabited by the energy of violence. Violence cannot be ended with violence. The Buddha said that responding to hatred with hatred can only increase hatred a thousandfold. Only by responding to hatred with compassion can we disintegrate hatred.

AFTER COMING TO the West in 1966 to call for a cessation to the war in Vietnam, I was not allowed by my government to go home. Suddenly I was cut off from all my friends, my students, my sangha in Vietnam. Almost every night I dreamed of going home. I would wake up in the middle of the dream and realize that I was in exile. During that time I practiced mindfulness diligently. I practiced to be in touch with children and adults in Europe and America. I learned to contemplate the trees and the singing of the birds. Everything seemed different from what we knew in Vietnam. And yet the wonders of life were available to me in these new lands, too. I came to the realization that, with the practice of mindfulness, my true home can be found everywhere on this planet.

I became aware that the Kingdom of God, the Pure Land of the Buddha, the place of true peace depends on our own capacity to wake up to all the wonders of life that surround us right in this moment, in this place. It is possible for us to touch the Kingdom of God every day and to regain the strength and hope to repair the damage caused by violence and war. It is possible, and it is up to us to do it. If we do not, we will be the victims of despair. We are never exiles from the place of true peace, the Kingdom of God or the Pure Land of the Buddha. I often tell my students, Come back and claim your true inheritance. Return to your true home, in the here and now, in the Kingdom of God, in the Pure Land of the Buddha. With just one mindful step, with just one mindful breath we can find ourselves in our paradise, where there is peace, understanding, and compassion.

Honoring Our Humanity

Although the place of true peace exists within each of us, the seed of violence that we also contain within us can sometimes overgrow and choke the seed of compassion. That violent seed when over-watered can give rise to the weed of terrorism. To uproot it, we first have to look at what anchors its roots. Do we even know where and what terrorism is? Can we pinpoint it with our radar? Terrorism lies in the hearts of human beings. We may feel we have to attack others so they will not be able to terrorize us, but the result of these actions may be the opposite of our goal of safety; it may lead to an escalation of terrorism. If we kill the terrorist father, the son may become a terrorist; the more we kill, the more terrorists we may create. That has been the course of history.

This is exactly what we do not want to do. We really want to uproot terrorism. We do not want to kill people—we want to kill terrorism, the disease of ignorance and misunderstanding within them.

Some people commit acts of terrorism in the name of God,

or in the name of their values and beliefs. Terrorists may be motivated by the belief that they are on the right side and that their spiritual values are threatened. They hold the view that the other side represents evil, and that they are justified in destroying their enemies in the name of God. We try to destroy them so they will have no opportunity to terrorize us. Terrorists die with the conviction that they are dying for a good cause, for God, for goodness. Are we not acting out of the same conviction when we kill terrorists? This action is motivated by fear.

Military force is one option, but there are better, more effective ways to end terrorism, at home and abroad. The United States relies too often on military force to resolve issues because she has not yet been trained to use the forces of understanding, compassion, and reconciliation. It is not with military might but with the practice of looking deeply into the human condition that terrorism will be ended.

Everyone wants to feel safe and protected. No one wants to live in fear day and night. Safety is a deep, basic wish of all people, no matter what race or nationality. Fear gives rise to violence. When we practice looking deeply, we will see that if the other people do not feel safe, then we will not have safety either. To secure safety for ourselves, we have to think about the safety of others. If we give others the impression that they are in danger, then we will be in danger, too. If we continue to create danger and instability for the other group, the danger will rebound on us. What we do to the other, we do at the same time to ourselves.

Safety is not an individual matter; it is a matter that concerns all of us. Happiness is like this, too. If your father is not happy, if he suffers deeply, there is no way you can be really happy. If your son suffers deeply, there is also no way you can really be happy. This is why thinking of the happiness of your son is thinking of your own happiness. Happiness and safety are alike. According to the practice of peace, you have to secure safety not just for yourself but for the other as well. This is true for all nations in the world. We need to work together to secure safety for everyone.

When you meditate on terrorism, you practice by meditating on this question: "You, the terrorist, must have suffered deeply, you must have a lot of hatred and anger toward us to do such a things. You have tried to destroy us, and you've caused us so much suffering. We want to understand why, to understand what is making you suffer. We want to know what kind of emotion, what kind of pain, what kind of misunderstanding has led you to such an action." Looking deeply is not a superficial action. It is an essential and crucial step in order to understand and recognize the roots of terrorism. Jesus said, "Love your enemies and pray for those who persecute you. If you only love those who love you, what reward do you have?"

As I have said, a doctor comes to help remove illness, not to kill the person who has been struck by illness. Martin Luther King Jr. said, "Through violence you murder the hater, but you do not murder the hate." Terrorists are human beings. They are sick with a virus called terrorism. Analyzing this virus, you see fear, misunderstanding, hate, and violence. When you act as a doctor, you do not kill the terrorist. Instead, you try to understand and transform the elements of terrorism in the terrorist's heart. And you do this knowing that this virus also exists in your own heart. A terrorist, like you, is a human being who has been heavily infected by the viruses of wrong perception and wrong belief. Terrorists suffer just as we do. Understanding this, we have the capacity to help them.

Nothing can help except the practice of restoring communication. If a doctor cannot talk to her patient, or if the patient refuses to cooperate, how can the doctor help the patient? "I refuse to recognize your insights as a doctor. You cannot help me." If the patient continues to feel this way, thinking, "This doctor is trying to kill me," then the patient will never be willing to work with the doctor, even if the doctor is motivated by a tremendous desire to help. The doctor cannot do anything without the patient's cooperation. That is why the first thing the doctor has to do is find ways to establish a relationship, lines of communication. If you can talk to the patient, there is hope. The patient will then accept and collaborate with the doctor. The doctor can then help to relieve the patient's suffering. Open communication between the parties will bring about mutual understanding.

The Land of True Peace

In Plum Village, we have three hamlets. In each hamlet there is a lotus pond. Every summer if you come you will see beautiful lotus flowers. In order for the lotus to grow, it needs mud. You cannot plant a lotus on marble, you have to plant it in mud. Looking into the lovely, fragrant lotus flower, you see the mud. Mud and lotus flowers inter-are. Without one the other cannot be, that is the teaching of the Buddha. This is because that is. Suffering is needed for understanding and compassion to be born, like garbage is necessary for flowers to be. Looking into a flower, you see that it is made only of non-flower elements: sunshine, rain, earth, the minerals, and also the compost. You see that the element of garbage is one of the non-flower elements that have helped the flower to manifest herself. If you are a good practitioner, looking into the flower you can see the garbage in it in the here and the now, just as you can see the sunshine and the rain in it. If you remove the sunshine from the flower, there will be no flower. If you remove the rain from the flower, the flower cannot be there. If you remove the garbage from the flower, then the flower also cannot be there. Look at the beautiful lotus flower. If you remove the mud from it, it cannot be there for you. This is because that is.

Our practice every day as bodhisattvas in training is to accept suffering and to learn to transform that suffering into hope, love, and compassion. We practice exactly like organic gardeners. They know that it is possible to transform garbage back into flowers. Let us learn to look at our suffering and the suffering of our world as a kind of compost. From that mud we can create the beautiful, fragrant lotuses of understanding and compassion. The flowers of understanding and compassion are already there in our hearts and minds in the form of seeds. Together we can practice to cultivate the flowers of understanding and compassion so that they can manifest every day for our happiness and well-being and the happiness and well-being of everyone around us.

I am sure that everyone has had the feeling that true peace, the Kingdom of God, the Pure Land of the Buddha is very close. One morning while doing walking meditation, I picked up a branch of flowers on the path in front of meditation hall and gave it to a monk who was on my left. I told him, "This belongs to the

Pure Land of the Buddha. Only the Pure Land of the Buddha has such a beautiful branch of flowers. Only the Kingdom of God has such a miracle as this branch of flowers." The blue skies, the beautiful vegetation, the lovely face of your child, the song of the birds, all these things belong to the Pure Land of the Buddha. If we are free enough, we can step into the Kingdom of God and enjoy walking in it. Every day it is my practice to enjoy walking in the Kingdom of God, to enjoy walking in the Pure Land of the Buddha. Even as I am aware that suffering, anger, and hatred are there, it is still possible for me to walk in the Kingdom of God every day. For me, the Kingdom of God is not a place where there is no suffering and violence. Rather, the Kingdom of God is a place where there is compassion, understanding, and love. There is no day when I do not enjoy walking in the Kingdom of God.

Every step should bring me peace and joy, which I need in order to continue my work—my work of building brotherhood, understanding, and compassion. Without that kind of nourishment, how can I continue? Go back to the present moment. Become fully alive. Don't run anymore. Get in touch with the wonders of life that are available. This is the basic practice of peace. If we can do that, we will have enough strength and joy to repair the damage caused by war, by violence and hatred, by misunderstanding. And we will know exactly how to live our daily life in order not to contribute to the kind of action that leads to more discrimination and more war, to more violence. Live in such a way that you embody true peace, that you can be peace in every moment of your daily life. It is possible for everyone to generate the energy of peace in every step. When you are able to touch the

Kingdom of God, to get in touch with the wonders of life that are available in the here and the now, you easily release everything else. You do not want to run anymore.

We have been running after the objects of our desire—fame, profit, and power. We thought they were essential to our happiness, but we have realized that our running has brought us a lot of suffering. We have not had the chance to live, to love and take care of our loved ones, because we cannot stop running. We run even when we sleep. That is why the Buddha advises us to stop. According to the teaching, it is possible to be happy right here and now. Going back to the here and the now with your mindful breathing and mindful walking, you will recognize many conditions of happiness that are already available.

The future is a notion. The future is made of only one substance, the present. If you are taking good care of the present moment, why do you have to worry about the future? By taking care of the present, you are doing everything you can to assure a good future. Is there anything else you can do? Live the present moment in such a way that peace and joy may be possible here and now—that love and understanding may be possible. Dwelling happily and peacefully in the present moment is the best thing we can do to ensure peace and happiness in the future.

We have to practice looking deeply as a nation if we want to get out of this difficult situation of war and terrorism. Our practice will help the other nations to practice. I am sure that America is very capable of punishing. The United States can send bombs; the whole world knows she is very capable of doing so. But America is great when she acts with lucidity and compassion. I urge that when we are suffering, when we are overcome by shock, we should not do anything, we should not say anything. We should go home to ourselves and practice mindful breathing and mindful walking to allow ourselves to calm down and to allow lucidity to come, so we can understand the real roots of our suffering and the suffering of the world. Only with that understanding can compassion arise. America can be a great nation if she knows how to act with compassion instead of punishment. We can offer peace. We can offer the relief of transformation and healing.

It is my deep wish that the American people and the people of other countries become spiritual allies and practice compassion together. Without a spiritual dimension and practice, we cannot really improve the situation of the world. We can come together as a family in order to look deeply into our own situation and the situation of the world.

Practicing peace is possible with every step, with every breath. It is possible for us to practice together and bring hope and compassion into our daily lives and into the lives of our families, our community, our nation, and the world.

MEDITATION FOR NONVIOLENCE

Let us offer the world the best flowers and fruits of our practice: lucidity, solidity, brotherhood, understanding, and compassion. Let us give rise to the determination to look deeply into the nature of fear, anger, hatred, and violence and to give rise to the eyes of compassion. Breathing in, I am aware of violence within myself and within the world. Breathing out, I am determined to look with the eyes of compassion at the violence within myself and within the world.

In this very moment, we invoke all of our spiritual teachers to be with us, to help us embrace the suffering of our nation. We ask them to embrace the entire world as one nation, to embrace humanity as a family. We ask their help as we become lucid and calm, so that we know exactly what to do and what not to do. We know that many people at this very moment are trying to rescue others, to support them, to ease their suffering. Let us be there for all of them and embrace them tenderly with all our compassion, understanding, and awareness. We know that with the energy of mindfulness, concentration, and awakened wisdom, we can practice to lessen violence every day. We know that responding to violence with compassion is our only path.

Let us bring our attention to our in breath and our out breath. We are aware of the presence of all our spiritual ancestors within us, supporting and guiding us to go on the path of nonviolence, understanding, and compassion.

EPILOGUE

A NEW GLOBAL ETHIC

The United Nations has declared the decade 2001–2010 the International Decade for the Culture of Peace and Non-violence for the Children of the World. It is a declaration of a new global ethic and expresses a universal desire and commitment to live in a way that promotes peace, stability, and growth for our children and our children's children. It also expresses the deep aspirations of many people of different cultures and faiths who came together to combine their understanding and spiritual traditions to work toward an ethic by which everyone can abide, one that can be accepted by all religious traditions.

With the declaration, the UN circulated a manifesto that provides guidelines for peacemaking based on the awareness that each of us depends on the well-being of the entire human population.

More than 75 million people, including heads of state from many countries, have signed the text. By signing, they have made the commitment to cultivate nonviolence and peace in themselves and in the world. You too can take part in this global endeavor. We can all grow in our awareness and encourage others to become involved by circulating the manifesto among our families, friends, and colleagues.

UNESCO™ MANIFESTO 2000
For a Culture of Peace and Non-violence

BECAUSE the year 2000 must be a new beginning, an opportunity to transform altogether the culture of war and violence into a culture of peace and non-violence,

BECAUSE this transformation demands the participation of each and every one of us, and must offer young people and the future generations values that can inspire them to shape a world based on justice, solidarity, liberty, dignity, harmony, and prosperity for all,

BECAUSE the culture of peace can underpin sustainable development, environmental protection, and the well-being of each person,

BECAUSE I am aware of my share of the responsibility for the future of humanity, in particular to the children of today and tomorrow, I pledge in my daily life, in my family, in my work, my community, my country, and my region to:

FIRST: *Respect all life.* Respect the life and dignity of each human being without discrimination or prejudice.

SECOND: *Reject violence.* Practice active non-violence, rejecting violence in all its forms: physical, sexual, psychological, economical, and social, in particular, towards the most deprived and vulnerable, such as children and adolescents.

THIRD: *Share with others.* Share my time and material resources in a spirit of generosity to put an end to exclusion, injustice, and political, and economic oppression.

FOURTH: *Listen to understand.* Defend freedom of expression and cultural diversity, giving preference always to dialogue and listening without engaging in fanaticism, defamation, and rejection of others.

FIFTH: *Preserve the planet.* Promote consumer behavior that is responsible and development practices that respect all forms of life and preserve the balance of nature on the planet.

SIXTH: *Rediscover solidarity.* Contribute to the development of my community, with the full participation of women and respect for democratic principles, in order to create together new forms of solidarity.

To manifest my personal contribution to promote a Culture of Peace and Non-violence, I undertake to:

_____

_____

_____

_____

_____

Signature:_____

Date:_____

First Name:_____

Surname:_____

Age:_____

Sex: M / F

Address:_____

_____

_____

_____

Town:_____

Zip/Postal Code:_____

Country:_____

Send to: Manifesto 2000
UNESCO
P.O. Box 3
91167 Longjumeau Cedex 9
FRANCE

ABOUT THE AUTHOR

The Venerable Thich Nhat Hanh is a world-renowned writer, scholar, spiritual leader, and Zen Buddhist monk. Since age sixteen, in fact, he has been a Buddhist monk, a peace activist, and a seeker of the Way. He has survived two wars in Vietnam and more than thirty years of exile from his native country, after he was banned by both the non-Communist and Communist governments for his role in establishing service groups to deal peacefully with the violence he saw affecting his people. He is still master of one of the most prominent temples in Vietnam, and his lineage is traceable directly to the Buddha.

Thich Nhat Hanh first gained world attention during the war in Vietnam, when he worked tirelessly for reconciliation between North and South Vietnam and led the Paris Peace Talks' Buddhist delegation. Driven by the destruction and chaos he saw around him, he set up relief organizations to rebuild destroyed villages, instituted the School of Youth for Social Service, founded a peace magazine, and urged world leaders to use nonviolence as a tool. His lifelong efforts to generate peace moved Martin Luther King Jr. to nominate him for the Nobel Peace Prize in 1967.

Thich Nhat Hanh is a visible proponent of "Engaged Buddhism," which links traditional meditative practices with active nonviolent civil disobedience. He is a universal spiritual leader whose mission it is to translate Buddhist precepts into everyday language and messages that everyone can understand. His career as a world leader and spiritual guide continues to grow; a prolific author, Thich Nhat Hanh has written more than one hundred books of philosophy, poetry, and fiction.

Currently Thich Nhat Hanh lives in Plum Village, a monastic community in southwestern France that he founded, as well as the center he founded in Vermont, Green Mountain Dharma Center, and Deer Park Monastery in Escondido, California, where he teaches, writes, gardens, and works to help refugees worldwide. Called Thay (pronounced "Tie"), an honorific meaning "teacher," by his thousands of students, he conducts retreats throughout the world on the art of mindful living and has conducted special retreats for American Vietnam War veterans, psychotherapists, artists, environmental activists, and children. More information can be found at www.plumvillage.org; email deerpark@plumvillage.org.

Information for Thich Nhat Hanh's Practice Centers

Plum Village
13 Martineau
33580 Dieulivol
France

or

Meyrac
47120 Loubes-Bernac
France
email: UH-Office@plumvillage.org.

USA Maples Forest Monastery/
Green Mountain Dharma Center
Ayers Lane
South Meadow Farm, VT 05041
USA
email: mfmaster@vermontel.net

Deer Park Monastery
2499 Melru Lane
Escondido CA 92026
USA
email: deerpark@plumvillage.org